THE MAXIMALLY EFFICIENT AND OPTIMALLY EFFECTIVE EMERGENCY DEPARTMENT

RADE B. VUKMIR

Dichotomy Press
Sewickley, PA

Dichotomy Press
www.dichotomypress.com

Sewickley
Pennsylvania 15143

The Maximally Efficient and Optimally Effective Emergency Department

Library of Congress Control Number: 2015917581

ISBN: 978-1-944351-12-0 (Hardcover)
ISBN: 978-1-944351-13-7 (Paperback)
eISBN: 978-1-944351-14-4 (Electronic)

DICHOTOMY
— PRESS —

For My Mom

Leni B. Vukmir

Disclaimer

The medical recommendations, although evidence-based, are meant to be suggested guidelines, and should not be interpreted as standards of care.

Contents

Preface

The emergency department (ED) perhaps more than any other hospital care unit—save for the operating room (OR)—drives the efficiency of the remainder of the hospital services. This is a complex effect, factoring in both operational, functional and economic aspects of this interface.

A structured, stepwise analysis is helpful to understanding. The process begins with analysis of patient triage, followed by registration, demographic analysis, patient processing, physician/midlevel efficiency, nursing/ancillary staff, data processing, physical plant analysis, admission process, consultation process, discharge, and special consideration for teaching hospitals.

Last and most important is the administrative vision and support required to make the operation a resounding success.

Chapter 1

Introduction

Every emergency department (ED) strives to attain an optimal level of effectiveness, while trying to achieve its valid patient care mission. There are numerous factors that affect the departmental operation. The most prominent issues obviously include the patient number, acuity and rapidity of presentation, balanced by staff and bed availability—both in the ED—as well as hospital admission bed vacancy.

An important consideration is that these factors are intimately intertwined so that a delay in one portion of the care chain involves other aspects of care as well.

The key to emergency medicine is "parallel process thinking" rather than series patient management (Figure 1). This concept is analogous to the physics of electrical circuitry allowing an alternative pathway for delivery if an impedance to flow is encountered. This attribute allows multiple tasks to be addressed simultaneously rather than sequentially.

Figure 1. Patient Management

Series

$$1 \quad 2 \quad 3$$
$$A \rightarrow B \rightarrow C \rightarrow D$$

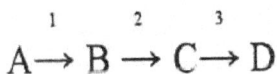

Patients seen in sequence
without deviations

Parallel

A B C D

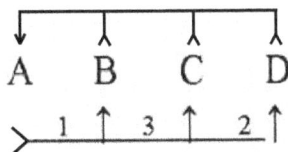

Sequence altered for emergency
concerns

Empowering each member of the staff to contribute and offer insight to the process will pay long term dividends to the institution. The "Team Approach" for all health care providers encourages tangible participation and "buy in" to the process. The quickest way to disenfranchise the group is to offer oversight and protocols without their input into the patient care process they perform involved in this care.

The best-run emergency departments, therefore, provide a proper balance of effectiveness of patient care accompanied by the maximization of the efficiency of the health care delivery system providing that care.

The consultation industry has a tendency to focus on *efficacy* with a theoretic constructive of work output that is untested—an abstract goal, if you will. This concept is in contrast to *effectiveness* or the actual work product in real life working conditions (Figure 2).

Figure 2. Work Productivity Measures

Efficacy—   The ability to bring out the desired endpoint under ideal conditions

Effectiveness— The ability to bring about the desired endpoint in real world conditions

Efficiency—   The ratio of work output fractioned by the resource input required

Therefore, the reference point for effectiveness must be contemporaneous actual clinical experience. Occasional observations of work interactions that are in the distant past are not productive or accurate.

Lastly, the concept of *efficiency* balancing the work product with the resources consumed is the most critical analysis point for the discussion.

This philosophy is tempered by the incorporation of a service excellence customer service model addressing the two areas of most concern: the timing of the visit and the amount of "caring" exhibited by the staff.[1]

This approach culminates in the "maximally efficient emergency department," providing both optimal patient care and customer-focused efficient care delivery (Figure 3).

Figure 3. Optimal Balance

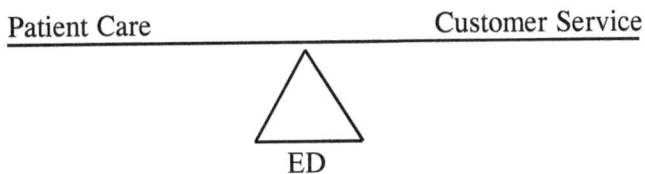

Patient Care   Customer Service

ED

References

1. Vukmir, R.B. "Customer satisfaction." *International Journal of Health Care Quality Assurance Incorporating Leadership in Health Services* 2006; 19(1): 8–31.

Chapter 2

Patient Intake Process

The reasons that patients present to the ED are varied and based on a host of factors including resources, education, efficiency and convenience. There is a commonly held belief that excessive ED use is found in high-risk populations.

One program offering extensive resources included a "Foster Grandmother" to assist at home, 40 hours per week of follow up clinic care and unlimited access to the physician assistant (PA) or nurse practitioner (NP), and free taxi service to a cohort of inner city high risk neonates factoring in either low birth weight of assisted ventilation requirement.[1]

These ED visits were tracked for a full year after many received instructions to help recognize early signs of illness. They reported ED visits for 52% of children with multiple visits found in one quarter. The moms remembered that fever is a worrisome sign in 75% of cases, but two-thirds could recall none of the other signs of illness and one-fifth could not offer any sign of illness on presentation to the ED.

The process variables were sub-optimal as well, with half of the visits involving parents not contacting their pediatric PA/NP prior to the visit, one-third of visits were for minor problems, 40% of visits were capable of clinic care, and the average interval of illness was 42 hours prior to presentation.

Clearly, focusing on this disappointing study alone, in which the families were provided maximal resources to avoid ED use, would have us conclude that an unremediable problem exists.

However, on a more positive note, the Emergency Medicine Patient's Access To Healthcare (EMPATH) Study explored behavior in a more empowered population. Here, the mean patient age was 46 years, the group was 55% female, and 81% of those studied had health insurance.[2]

The rationale for presentation was medical necessity (95%) followed by convenience (87%), citing hours of operation, ease of travel, and availability of immediate medical attention and preference (89%) for ED use. Analysis found that financial reasons were cited less often in this population, specifically affordability (25%) and insurance limitations (15%).

The "preference of the ED" descriptor involves four factors: the environment and staffing of the ED, the availability of a wide range of services at a single site, the availability of diagnostic testing and the availability of specialty consultants (Figure 4).

Figure 4. Why the Affirmative Choice of the Emergency Department
1. Environment and staffing of the ED.
2. Availability of services at a single site.
3. Wide range of diagnostic testing.
4. Availability of specialty consultants.

Reference 2

Clearly, the ED can be viewed as an "affirmative choice" in some patient populations rather than just the "last resort" in less advantaged patient groups.

The patient intake process is often complicated by the referral of "elective" patients blending with the ED population. The mix between acute and elective patients proves especially difficult during high saturation times in the department due to triage inadequacies. Triage agreement can be notoriously poor. An evaluation of emergent (15%), urgent (44%) and routine (41%) patients finds substantial agreement in only 1 of 5 cases and the overall level of agreement (kappa=0.35) was poor.[3]

Therefore, the needle-in-the-haystack approach to finding the 'sick' patient in triage should be avoided. A multifaceted system is required in the sea of routine patient processing tasks. A helpful approach is to set reasonable patient expectations, explaining morning/early day accessibility versus afternoon or evening/late day lack of processing capability as well as the necessity of 'calling ahead' by office personnel to allow the ED staff time to budget accordingly.

These patients are typically referred by their physicians' offices due to the convenience of STAT testing without the conventional laboratory wait time. This practice can interfere with the routine ED triage and the flow of more critically ill patients.

A more efficient approach would be to rotate these referred patients to a separate holding area or waiting area to await the results of non-critical testing. The referring physicians of those patients who warrant admission would be directed to the Direct Emergency Admission (DEA) pathway[4] (Figure 5).

This pathway allows a nursing vital sign evaluation and floor transfer to a waiting bed, where the lab and x-ray personnel could also be alerted. The radiology department can be visited during the transfer process and laboratory specimens can be obtained on bed arrival.

The referral of patients from their doctor's office—often due to lack of appointment availability—causes perhaps the most significant inequity encountered in the system. This problem manifests itself in two variants. The first involves the referring office's clerical staff who may not have a vested interest in seeing additional patients. The compliant patients who have followed their doctor's advice to "call the office, not just go to the emergency room (ER)," are then instructed to "go to the ER."

The second variant has the same endpoint for the patient but emanates from the physician or midlevel provider—"since you have 'blank' condition or need 'blank' test you need to go to the ED, otherwise we could see you in the office."

Here, a helpful approach is to suggest that practitioners use a recommended office emergency appointment availability allotment time. Another approach is the "open office" with the flex capacity to see all patients who desire to be seen. This approach may allocate anywhere from 5 to 10% of office appointment availability to this patient population which often present—especially in peak seasons related to infectious disease outbreaks or regarding routine health needs, such as school physicals and vaccinations.

An interesting paradox is that some office-based practitioners might muse that they could never see such an influx of patients with their current office staff, but recognize that we would then expect the ED staff to perform the same task, while having to take care of true emergencies as well.

The last issue is usually a physician-based decision as well, where patients are referred to the ER for "difficult procedures." These tend to

Figure 5. Direct Emergent Admission (DEA) Protocol

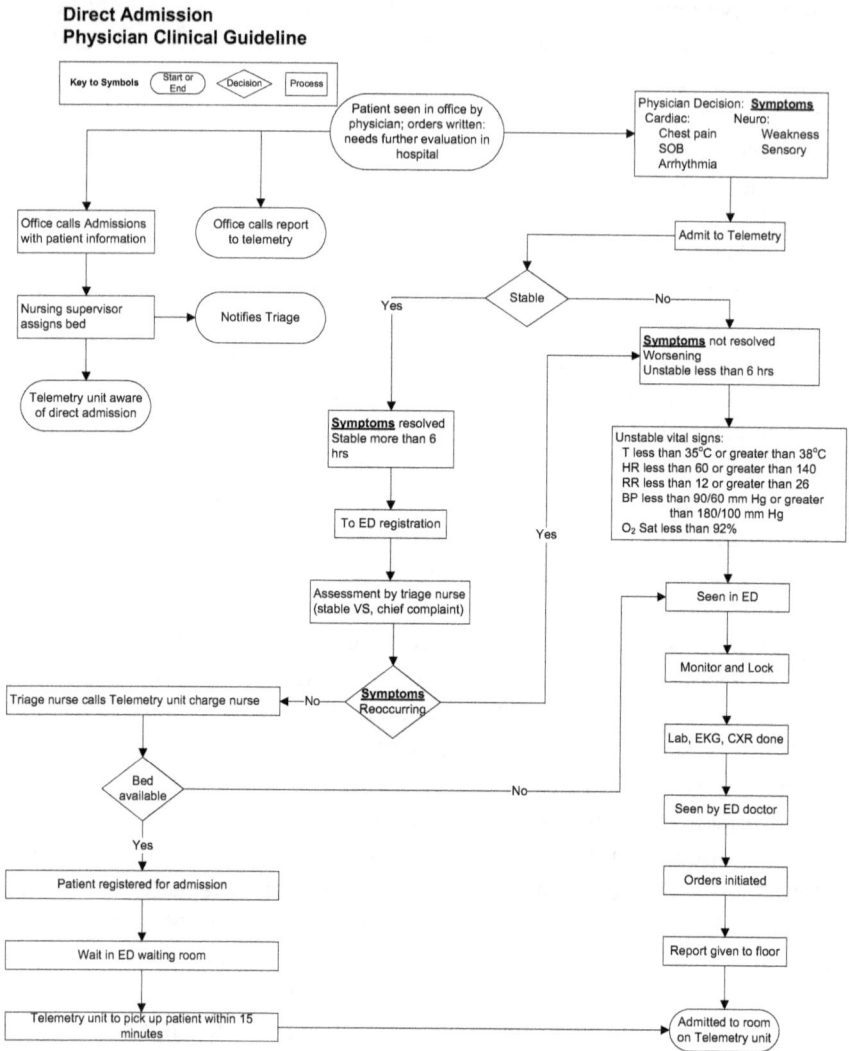

**Direct Admission
Physician Clinical Guideline**

Key to Symbols — Start or End — Decision — Process

Patient seen in office by physician; orders written: needs further evaluation in hospital

Physician Decision: **Symptoms**
Cardiac:　　　Neuro:
　Chest pain　　Weakness
　SOB　　　　　Sensory
　Arrhythmia

Office calls Admissions with patient information

Office calls report to telemetry

Admit to Telemetry

Nursing supervisor assigns bed → Notifies Triage

Stable — Yes / No

Telemetry unit aware of direct admission

Symptoms not resolved
Worsening
Unstable less than 6 hrs

Symptoms resolved
Stable more than 6 hrs

Unstable vital signs:
T less than 35°C or greater than 38°C
HR less than 60 or greater than 140
RR less than 12 or greater than 26
BP less than 90/60 mm Hg or greater than 180/100 mm Hg
O$_2$ Sat less than 92%

To ED registration

Yes

Assessment by triage nurse (stable VS, chief complaint)

Seen in ED

Monitor and Lock

Triage nurse calls Telemetry unit charge nurse — No — **Symptoms** Reoccurring

Lab, EKG, CXR done

Bed available — No

Seen by ED doctor

Yes

Patient registered for admission

Orders initiated

Wait in ED waiting room

Report given to floor

Telemetry unit to pick up patient within 15 minutes

Admitted to room on Telemetry unit

Rade B. Vukmir, M.D., JD, FCCP, FACEP

Emergency Consultants, Inc.© 1999-2006

Revised April 2006

Reference 4

be interventions that are time consuming, work intensive or subject to skill attrition. These procedures include lumbar punctures, alleged child abuse evaluations, alleged sexual assault evaluations, gynecologic exams, or involuntary commitment procedures.

Here, it is helpful to maintain select procedural competence in physicians, requiring doctor-to-doctor referral, because these transfers utilize other procedural-based specialties, specifically radiology and anesthesia personnel for requested procedures such as lumbar puncture. Likewise, the office staff should be familiar with the procedural requirements of other public service agencies for certain forensic patient examinations, such as those required for an alleged sexual assault evaluation, for instance.

Obviously, these considerations are factored into the ED operating plan and are incorporated into the average daily patient evaluation plan. If peak use times are encountered in the ED, alternate suggested referral patterns are helpful to the primary care physicians (PCPs) to ensure that their patients are seen as well, utilizing hospital resources other than the emergency department to get these goals accomplished.

References

1. Hoffmann, C., Broyles, R.S., Tyson, J.E. "Emergency room visits despite the availability of primary care: A Study of High Risk Inner City Infants." *American Journal of the Medical Sciences* 1997; 313(2): 99–103.

2. Ragin, D.F., Hwang U., Cydulka, R.K., Holson, D., Haley, L.L. Jr., Richards, C.F., Becker, B.M., Richardson, L.D. "Reasons for using the emergency department: results of the EMPATH Study." *Academy of Emergency Medicine* 2005; 12: 1158–66.

3. Wuerz, R., Fernandes, C.M., Alarcon, J. "Inconsistency of emergency department triage. Emergency Department Operations Research Working Group." *Annals of Emergency Medicine* 1998; 32(4): 431–5.

4. Emergency Consultants Inc.© Vukmir, R., O'Rourke, I. *QualChart Information Systems Patient Management Program*. Traverse City, MI. Revision 4.04; 2005–2006.

Chapter 3

Registration Process

The patient care process begins with registration and, with the advent of the information age, registration has taken on even greater importance than ever. (Figure 6)

The registration personnel are often quite adept at helping to detect 'who is sick.' The staffing model utilizes 0.4–0.5 registration hours per patient visit. This compares to the 1.7–2.1 productive nursing hours per patient visit (hppv).[1] Therefore, compared to the nursing equivalent, good registration personnel require 25–33% of the time to perform their part of the patient care continuum.

The managed care interface has been exponentially difficult for some patients and providers to navigate successfully. The major manifestations of this are in the difficulty in accessing physicians as well as long appointment waits and testing delays.

The patients have adapted to this scenario by utilizing the emergency department. "If you have to go to the ER, you don't need an appointment, can get your testing done, can even receive medication there as well and even return transportation." Some patients will make this decision, suggesting that this one-stop convenience outweighs the detriment of the co-pay for those that have insurance, and has minimal impact for those that don't.

Often times the ED staff can assist with scheduling the desired testing as outpatient procedures, thus avoiding admission or further unnecessary delay. The first appointment for "next-day testing" is often helpful, assuming this slot is reserved for ED patients.

It is problematic when retrospective certification requirements are instituted after patients present for care. These "pre-certification" re-

Figure 6.   **Emergency Department Patient Processing Plan**

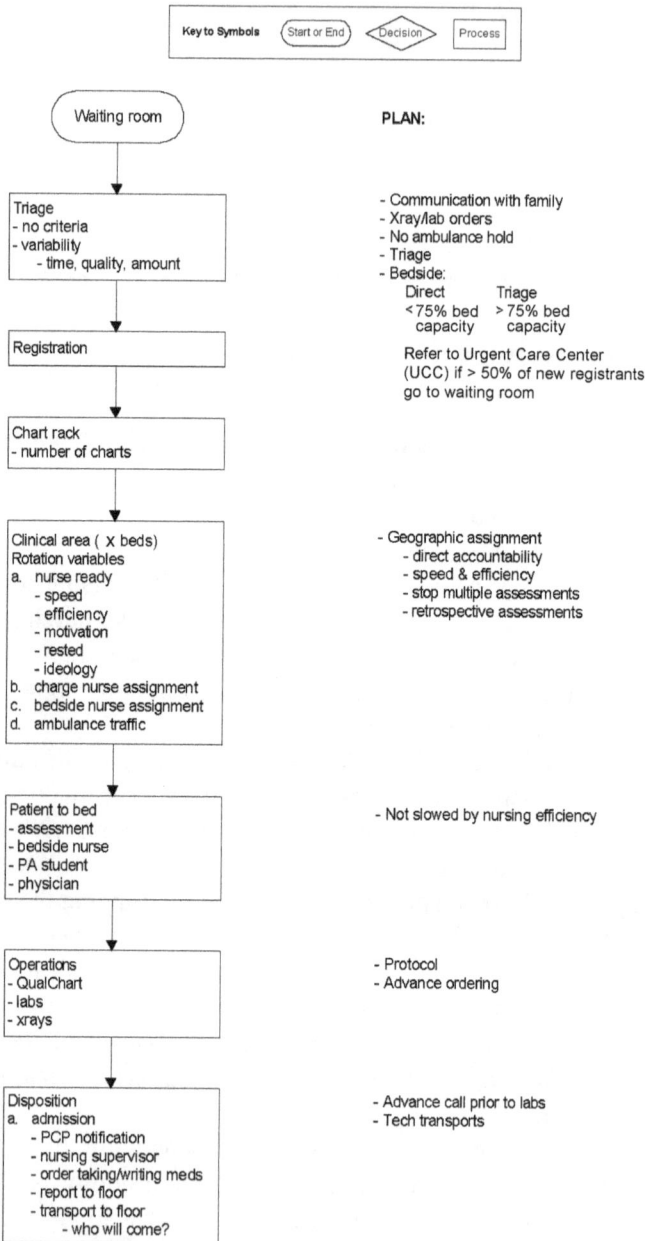

Key to Symbols (Start or End) ◇ Decision ◇ □ Process

Waiting room

PLAN:

Triage
- no criteria
- variability
    - time, quality, amount

- Communication with family
- Xray/lab orders
- No ambulance hold
- Triage
- Bedside:

Direct	Triage
< 75% bed	> 75% bed
capacity	capacity

Refer to Urgent Care Center
(UCC) if > 50% of new registrants
go to waiting room

Registration

Chart rack
- number of charts

Clinical area (X beds)
Rotation variables
a. nurse ready
    - speed
    - efficiency
    - motivation
    - rested
    - ideology
b. charge nurse assignment
c. bedside nurse assignment
d. ambulance traffic

- Geographic assignment
    - direct accountability
    - speed & efficiency
    - stop multiple assessments
    - retrospective assessments

Patient to bed
- assessment
- bedside nurse
- PA student
- physician

- Not slowed by nursing efficiency

Operations
- QualChart
- labs
- xrays

- Protocol
- Advance ordering

Disposition
a. admission
    - PCP notification
    - nursing supervisor
    - order taking/writing meds
    - report to floor
    - transport to floor
        - who will come?

- Advance call prior to labs
- Tech transports

Rade B. Vukmir, M.D., JD, FCCP, FACEP

Reference 2

quirements are often work-intensive administrative impediments that are established to ration the provision of select care. This arduous administrative burden often shifts to the often-overworked ED staff; the procedures are often associated with psychiatric issues or drug and alcohol use care, both of which are routinely rationed by the healthcare insurance providers. Since this information is best provided by the primary care physician or clinic, the difficulty often leads to a transition of this task to the emergency department staff.

To help speed patient disposition, a multidisciplinary approach to this dilemma can be helpful. Registration personnel can often contact case management or social service departments for "pre-certification" assistance early in the process of select cases. Likewise, the use of a psychiatric liaison could help to facilitate placement for mental healthcare.

Most facilities have some manner of registration impediment or "paperwork" bottleneck. Therefore, conversion to an integrated electronic registration system is essential to proper functioning. A bedside registration program should be initiated from the inception or when the ED is 50–75% occupied depending on the facility (Figure 7).

A novel approach analogous to the "Call-Ahead Seating" process can be attempted to help alleviate this difficulty. Here, the patients would register themselves at a secure web-based hospital registration site. There are two benefits offered by this novel registration process, where the patient receives an appointment time for select routine care issues. This alleviates ED overcrowding issue, while still offering a customer service solution to the "minor emergency" problem.

It is inherently obvious, however, that an integrated patient registration process is instrumental to the department's success.

Figure 7. Bedside Registration Protocol

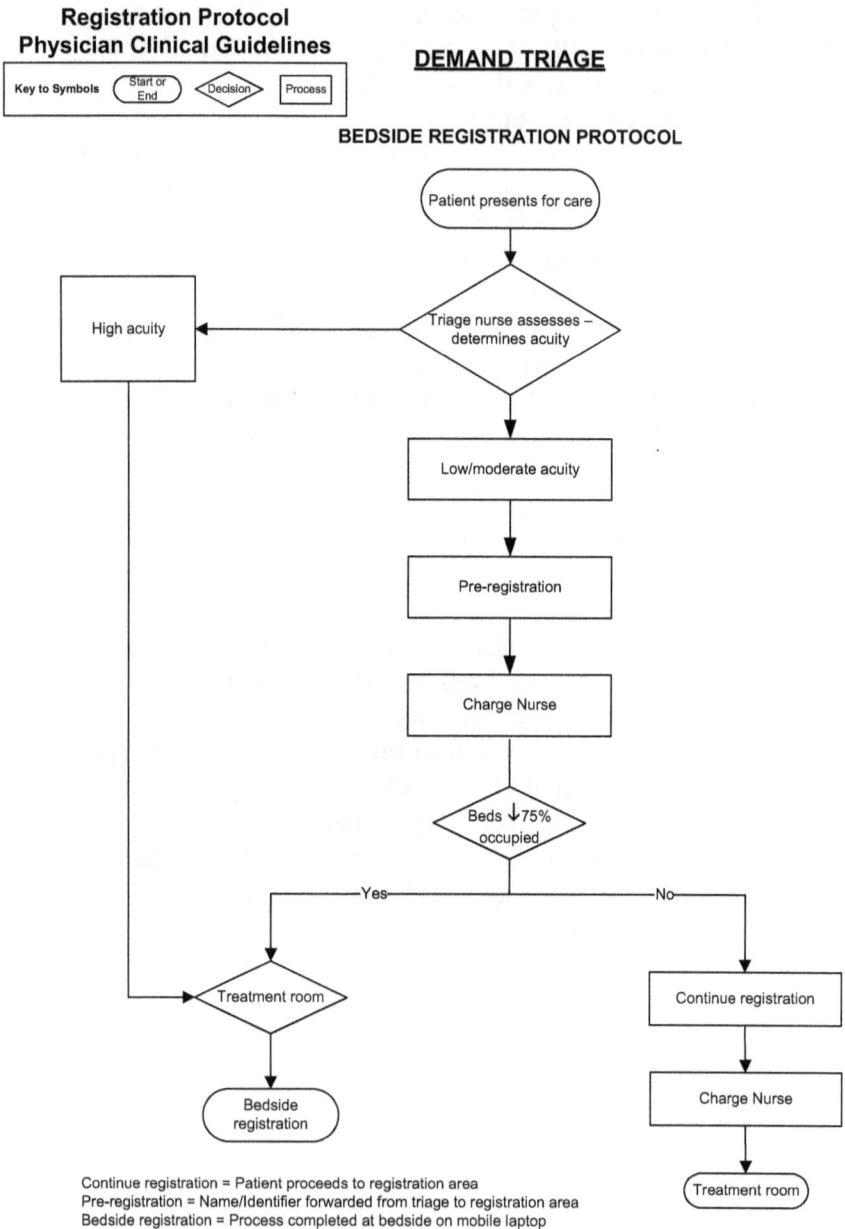

Registration Protocol
Physician Clinical Guidelines   **DEMAND TRIAGE**

Key to Symbols — Start or End / Decision / Process

BEDSIDE REGISTRATION PROTOCOL

Continue registration = Patient proceeds to registration area
Pre-registration = Name/Identifier forwarded from triage to registration area
Bedside registration = Process completed at bedside on mobile laptop

Rade B. Vukmir, MD, JD, FCCP, FACEP

Reference 2

Reference

1. "Benchmarking in Emergency Services." *ACEP Management Course Manual* 1994: 7

2. Emergency Consultants Inc.© Vukmir, R., O'Rourke, I. *QualChart Information Systems Patient Management Program.* Traverse City, MI. Revision 4.04; 2005–2006.

Chapter 4

Patient Demographics

A host of patient-based difficulties and solutions can be related to the diversity of patient predictors and associations specific to the ED population. Perhaps, the most ubiquitous trend is the steady increase in the number of patients presenting for care. The average ED experiences a 5–10% annual increase, with some facilities experiencing spikes of 25–30% patient volume increase per year. In addition, the patients are often sicker, older, and have less care resources available.[1]

Most EDs have already adapted to this trend, offering a midlevel provider to evaluate approximately 30% of patients, with a range of 20–40% of the total patient volume.[2] This trend has been met with improved patient satisfaction with a better matching of patient and provider expectation of care needs.

Secondly, there is a well-established progression toward a higher complexity of illness, as patients are unable—or in some cases unwilling—to receive preventive care. Office-based practitioners are often referring their more difficult cases associated with multiple treatments, interventions, and revisits to the emergency department for care as well.

These patients could be carrying their record of office-based interventions, as there could also be a call from their referring physician prior to evaluation. Often what occurs is that the office personnel recommends that they "go to the ER" with neither of the above taking place.

Thirdly, there is an increased proportion of uninsured patients who present to the ER as a societal "safety net" or de-facto universal health insurance coverage. (In fact, the "self pay" patients often times generate less revenue than is necessary to recover the cost of generating the bill for the service itself.)

An active case-management-based approach is often helpful—where nursing, social services or registration personnel are enlisted to encourage patient access and enrollment in public welfare programs. In fact, enrollment forms and interviews may be completed while waiting for care. This program should however be completed on the exit interview once the care intervention is complete to avoid any Emergency Medical Treatment And Labor Act (EMTALA) considerations (Figure 8).

Figure 8. Financial Enrollment Form

Patient Acct: REG ER
Patient Name:
Patient SSN: ______
Responsible Party Name: ______
Responsible Party SSN: ______

Dependents in Household
(This includes spouse, children under 18 and all others claimed on your tax return)

Dependent Name (First, Middle and Last Name if different than patient)	Age	Date of Birth	Social Security Number

Employment

	Patient / Responsible Party	Spouse
Employer name:		
Hourly Rate:		
Current Gross Weekly, Monthly or Yearly Income (Before Taxes):		
If unemployed, date last worked:		

Other Income

	Patient / Responsible Party	Spouse
Social Security		
Pension		
Unemployment		
Worker's Compensation		
VA Benefits		
Rental Income		
Stocks, Bonds, 401K		
Dividend / Interest		
Child Support		
Other		

Have you applied for Medicaid or any other State/County Assistance? ______

If yes and known. Case Number ______ Date Applied ______

I, the undersigned, certify that the above information is true and accurate to the best of my knowledge. I understand that the information submitted is subject to verification. In the review process, a credit report may be requested to verify information provided in this application. I understand that falsification of information submitted may jeopardize my consideration for the program. Furthermore, to qualify for this program, I understand I must apply for any and all assistance that may be available to help pay this hospital bill prior to completing this application.

Signature ______ Date ______

Fourth, language barriers become increasingly common, as the cultural diversity of this country increases. This trend results in difficulty with information transfer from patient to provider to help to facilitate proper diagnosis and treatment.

An interesting trial compared discharge instructions offered by the ED physician compared to a discharge clerk reading written instructions to English- (69%) and Spanish-speaking (31%) patients.[3] They found that 97% of English-speaking and 81% of Spanish-speaking patients indicated discharge information was adequately explained.

However, specific subgroups found differences in proper understanding of diagnosis in 83 vs. 61%, medication use in 39 vs. 12%, medicine-dosing schedules in 30 vs. 18%, and follow-up instructions in 74 vs. 57% of English- and Spanish-speaking patients respectively.

The most commonly used intervention—"the AT&T® Language Line"—is often time-consuming, difficult to access, and a potentially expensive approach (Figure 9). However, it is often the only possible approach in difficult situations with rare and unusual language needs.

Figure 9. Language Line

Based in Monterey California
1982 Volunteer Based in Santa Clara County
1989 AT&T® acquired, 2004 ABRY Partners
Services Government, Health Care, Telecom
175 Languages
24 Hours/7 Days/No Appointment

Translation tools are available to help process computerized files and information into Spanish, Portuguese, German, Dutch, French, and often less commonly used languages as well (Figure 10).

Figure 10. Language Translation Software

Any text file can be translated
Software—Excel, Powerpoint, Outlook, HTML
Plug-in dictionaries
Accurate; UTD Transactions

Spanish	German
Portuguese	Dutch
French	Italian
Swedish	Russian
Japanese	Korean
	Chinese—both traditional and simplified.

An on-site language data bank consisting of hospital personnel is often more effective and more personal. The convenient approach is to allow family translation, but this method is often problematic based on the potential for bias or information processing by the family. Unfortunately, this situation is often exacerbated if young children (often born here) are listed as "translators." They are often helpful and try to please; however, sophisticated analysis may be beyond their capacity to inform and communicate to their parents. It is an unfair burden to impose upon them.

Proactive approaches utilize computerized translation tools for speech and written language processing of patient medical records. There are programs currently in place that process discharge instructions in over 30 languages for the ED patient (Figure 11).

Language differences are just one manifestation of the growing culture divide engaging society today. This issue is manifested as the potential for race-, gender-, and class-based patient preferences for care is becoming more prominent. An additional concern is a true understanding of local and regional folk medicine interventions as well.

A survey of alternative medicine use found that from 1990 to 1999 the proportion of patients who saw an alternative medical provider increased by one-third from 36.3% to 46.3%.[4] There has been an increase in the use of herbal remedies by 380%, high-dose vitamins by 130%, and 1 in 5 patients (18.4%) use at least one of these products on a daily basis.

It is crucial to note that of the approximately one-third of patients who utilize alternative medicine therapy approaches, three-quarters do

Figure 11. Discharge Instructions

Discharge / Follow-Up Instructions
Please Follow Carefully

Provisional Diagnosis:

You may have received additional written instructions.
Please read and follow them carefully.

☐ Follow up with Dr. _____ or your Primary Care Physician. Please call his/her office for an appointment.
☐ An appointment has been made for you on: Date: _____ Time: _____
Additional
Instructions:
☐ Smoking cessation information has been provided.

The examination and treatment you have received in the Emergency Department have been given on an emergency basis only. If you do not seem to be improving, seem to be getting worse, or have any new symptoms, you should **return to the Emergency Department** or contact your Primary

If you had x-rays taken today: X-rays do not always show injury or disease immediately. Fractures (breaks in bones) do not always show up on the initial x-rays but may show on later x-rays. Your x-rays taken today have been read on a preliminary basis only. Final reading will be done by the radiologist, and you will be notified of any additional findings.

If lab tests were performed today: Some results may not be received for 24 - 72 hours. You will be contacted if there are any results requiring further testing or a change in treatment.

If you received stitches or staples: They should be removed in _____ days.

Work / School Release:
☐ May return to work/school immediately with no limitations.   ☐ Off work/school today, may return next scheduled shift/day.
☐ Off work/school for _____ days. Re-check by family/company doctor or preferred doctor prior to return recommended.
☐ May return to work/school with the following limitations:

I have a copy of these instructions. The doctor explained them to me and I understand them. I will follow the instructions that I have been given. I will take the medicine as told. I will see the doctor as told. I know this exam is only for my problem today. I may have other problems that need care. I also need normal medical care. I **will return to the Emergency Department** or contact my Primary Care Physician if I get worse, stay the same, or begin to have new symptoms.

_____   _____
Signature of patient or responsible party   Date

Name: _____   Date of Birth: _____
Address: _____   Date: _____

R_x

Name: _____   Date of Birth: _____
Address: _____   Date: _____

R_x

Refill _____ times

Refill _____ times

_____
Signature

_____
Signature

DEA #
Another brand of generically equivalent product, identical in dosage, form and content of active ingredients, may be dispensed unless box is initialed
D.A.W.   ☐

DEA #
Another brand of generically equivalent product, identical in dosage, form and content of active ingredients, may be dispensed unless box is initialed
D.A.W.   ☐

This form is to assist the physician's documentation of clinical care and treatment. It is not intended to supplant that judgment or create a standard of care.

Reference 5

Figure 11. Discharge Instructions (continued)

EMERGENCY DEPARTMENT
After-Care Instructions

ABDOMINAL COMPLAINT
(Belly Pain)

The Emergency Department doctor does not think that you need to stay in the hospital right now. This was decided based on what you told us about your symptoms, the examination by the doctor, and any tests that were done while you were in the Emergency Department.

What causes abdominal or belly pain?

Abdominal pain, sometimes called belly pain, is a symptom that can come from many different things, like: infection, gall bladder disease, liver disease, kidney disease, bladder infections, a woman's monthly period, tumors, ulcers, hernias, heart problems, etc. Even though some of these problems are not actually in your belly they can make your belly hurt.

How bad the pain is does not necessarily tell you how serious the problem causing the pain is. Very bad belly pain can be caused by things that are not serious, like gas or the cramps you have with viral gastroenteritis (sometimes called stomach flu), or diarrhea. You could also have mild pain (or no pain) but have a very serious problem, like early appendicitis. The exact cause of your belly pain might not be found while you are in the Emergency Department, but the Emergency Department doctor will make sure that the pain is not from anything serious that could cause permanent problems. Your regular family doctor might have to do more tests later to try to figure out why you are having pain.

Treatment recommendations:

- You should rest. You may do normal activities if you don't have pain.
- The doctor may give you medicine to help lessen the pain. Do not drive or do things that need your full attention after you take this medicine.
- Do not eat regular food until you feel better.
- Drink only clear liquids like juice, broth, or ginger ale for the next 12 to 24 hours.
- Do not drink coffee or drinks with caffeine. Do not drink alcohol.
- Once you are feeling better, you can eat a bland diet. Do not eat spicy or greasy foods.
- You should not take aspirin or ibuprofen-like medicines unless your doctor said that it is ok.

CONTACT YOUR DOCTOR OR RETURN TO THE EMERGENCY ROOM IF ANY OF THE FOLLOWING THINGS HAPPEN:

- Pain gets worse or is there all the time.
- You start to have fever or chills, especially if they don't go away after you take your medicines.
- You can't keep liquids or medicine down because of vomiting.
- There is blood in your vomit, urine (pee), or stool (poop).
- You start to have bad diarrhea.
- You start to have an unusual color to your skin, eyes, urine (pee), or stool (poop).
- Your belly becomes swollen or you stop having bowel movements (poop).
- Your belly is tender to touch, or it feels hard.
- You are not getting any better.
- Any other symptoms that seem unusual or worry you.
- If you start to have chest pain or trouble breathing you should call 911. **Do not try to drive yourself to the hospital.**

Revised 02/07

Reference 5

Figure 11. Discharge Instructions (continued)

> DEPARTAMENTO DE LA EMERGENCIA
> Instrucciones para el cuidado

QUEJA ABDOMINAL
(Dolor del vientre)

El médico del departamento de emergencia no considera que usted necesita ser admitido al hospital en este momento.Esta decisión fue basada en la descripción de los síntomas, de su examen, y de cualquier prueba que pudo habersido hecha mientras estaba en el departamento de emergencia.

¿Qué causa dolor abdominal o del vientre?

El dolor abdominal, a veces llamado dolor del vientre, es un síntoma que puede venir de muchas diversas causas, como: Infección, la enfermedad de la vesicular biliar, enfermedad del hígado, enfermedad del riñón, infecciones de la vejiga, el período menstrual en la mujer, tumores, úlceras, hernias, problemas del corazón, etc. aun cuando algunos de estos problemas no están realmente en el abdomen pueden afectarlo de igual manera.

La seriedad de un problema abdominal no se define necesariamente por la intensidad del dolor. Un cólico abdominal intenso puede ser causado por cosas que no son serias, como el gas o los calambres que usted tiene con la gastroenteritis viral (a veces llamada gripe del estómago), o la diarrea. Usted podría también tener un dolor mínimo (o ningún dolor) y todavía tener un problema muy serio, como apendicitis temprana. La causa exacta de su dolor abdominal podría no ser hallada durante su visita al departamento de emergencia, pero el doctor del departamento de emergencia se cerciorará de que su dolor no proviene de alguna causa seria que pudiera causarle problemas permanentes. Su médico primario quizás ordene más pruebas de laboratorio para tratar de encontrar la causa del dolor en su abdomen.

Recomendaciones del tratamiento:

- Repose en cama. Usted puede hacer actividades normales si no tiene dolor.
- El doctor puede darle una medicina para disminuir el dolor. No conduzca ni haga cosas que requieran su total atención después de tomar esta medicina.
- No coma su dieta regular hasta que se sienta definitivamente mejor.
- Beba solamente líquidos claros como jugos de frutas, caldo, o la cerveza inglesa de jengibre (Ginger Ale), por las próximas 12 a 24 horas.
- No beba el café o las bebidas con cafeína. No beba el alcohol.
- Una vez que usted se esté sintiendo mejor, usted puede comer una dieta suave. No coma alimentos picantes o grasientos.
- Usted no debe tomar medicamentos que contengan aspirina o ibuprofen a menos que su doctor diga que es aceptable.

COMUNIQUESE CON SU MEDICO O REGRESE AL DEPARTAMENTO DE EMERGENCIA SI OCURRE CUALQUIERA DE LO SIGUIENTE:

- El dolor empeora o no desaparece.
- Usted comienza a tener fiebre o escalofríos, especialmente si no mejoran después de que usted toma sus medicinas.
- Usted no puede retener líquidos o la medicina en su estomago, debido al vomito.
- Hay sangre en su vómito, orina o material fecal.

02/07 revisado
Página 1 de 2

Reference 5

Figure 11. Discharge Instructions (continued)

DEPARTAMENTO DE LA EMERGENCIA
Instrucciones para el cuidado

- Usted comienza a tener diarrea intensa.
- Usted comienza a tener un color inusual en su piel, ojos, orina o material fecal
- Su vientre se hincha o usted deja de tener movimientos intestinales.
- Su vientre duele al tocarlo, o se siente duro o tenso.
- Usted no está mejorando en absoluto.
- Cualquiera otros síntomas que le parezcan inusuales o que le preocupan.
- Si usted comienza a tener dolor en el pecho o dificultad respiratoria, usted debe llamar 911. **No intente conducir usted mismo hasta el hospital.**

Reference 5

not advise their physician of this practice.[4] Specifically, Chinese herbal remedies contain variable amounts of toxic alkaloids with 10–650 of these compounds proven toxic.[6] Since these medicines are unregulated, toxic heavy metal contaminants found in the products are also a problem.

There are often vast cultural, language, and communication gaps in day-to-day emergency medicine practice. An interview survey of an ED population of largely female (65%), Hispanic (78%) patients were evaluated by a male physician (61%). Female, but not male, patients were more likely to be satisfied, citing time spent, showing of concern, and trust; they gave an improved overall rating if they were treated by a female physician.[7]

Additional correlations found older patients more trusting than their younger counterparts. The cultural divide was manifested in the finding that those with lower levels of functional health literacy and Spanish-speaking patients without an interpreter were less satisfied as well.

A multimodal approach should be utilized to overcome this pervasive problem. An insightful practitioner will utilize similarities in medical staff personnel to bridge the gap. It is helpful to spend the initial interview time communicating a desire to understand all of life's circumstances to help with medical issues, including folk and alternative medicine approaches to disease. Mutual trust will certainly help to facilitate any care plan.

The patient-centered approach allowed the patient to elaborate on symptoms and concerns relevant to his condition. The physician then acted on the patient's expectations, thoughts, feelings, prompts, and non-specific signs. However, there was a difference in scores with more offers of discussion (20 vs. 7) for English- than Spanish-speaking patients, while patient-centered evaluation scores (1.1 vs. 0.6) were higher as well ($p < 0.001$).[8]

Sixth, sometimes with disadvantaged circumstances there may be an accompanying difficulty with personal responsibility exhibited by patients and families. This may manifest itself when the patients return to the ED "no better," but with unfilled prescriptions, physician referral visits and other recommendations not completed from the previous visit. This is often frustrating for the staff.

This issue is often more complex than lack of financial resources or funding that may have been expended for other purposes. This problem requires financial resource analysis by social service to facilitate delivery of the fungibles of care. However, the subtler aspect of the health care encounter is to help patients understand the care contract to help facilitate participation in their own health and recovery.

Seventh, there is another aspect of patient sophistication at the other extreme of the spectrum. There are some patients that are hypervigilant, offering internet research, books, magazine articles, and friends' advice on their care. The evidence-based standards on your part will encourage them to participate in a shared mutual plan of care, increasing buying and the likelihood of success. Rather than resenting the patient's or family's "internet" research, you should encourage and help to facilitate their participation. They will soon become a strong ally in the healthcare partnership, as they can inform the other family members of your findings.

References

1. "Institute of Medicine of the National Academies: Report Brief." *The future of emergency care in the United States Health System* 2006; 1–8.

2. Hooker, R.S. *Non-physician clinicians: The US experience international Medical workforce conference.* Oxford, England. September 2002; 1–2.

3. Crane, J.A. "Patient Comprehension of doctor-patient communication on discharge from the emergency department." *Journal of Emergency Medicine* 1997; 15(1): 1–7.

4. Eisenberg, D.M., Davis, R.B., Ettner, S.L., Appel, S., Wilkey, S., Van Rompay, M., Kessler, R.C. "Trends in alternative medicine use in the United States, 1990–1997: results of a follow-up national survey." *Journal of the American Medical Association* 1998; 280(18): 1569–75.

5. Emergency Consultants Inc.© Vukmir, R., O'Rourke, I. *QualChart Information Systems Patient Management Program.* Traverse City, MI. Revision 4.04; 2005–2006.

6. Bateman, J., Chapman, R.D., Simpson, D. "Possible toxicity of herbal remedies." *Scottish Medical Journal* 1998; 43(1): 7–15.

7. Derose, K.P., Hays, R.D., McCaffrey, D.F., Baker, D.W. "Does physician gender affect satisfaction of men and women visiting the emergency department?" *Journal of General Internal Medicine* 2001; 16(4): 218–26.

8. Rivadeneyra, R., Elderkin-Thomason, V., Silver, R.C., Waitzkin, H. "Patient centeredness in medical encounters requiring an interpreter." *American Journal of Medicine* 2000; 108(6): 470–4.

Chapter 5

Patient Processing-Lab and X-ray

An especially integral part of the ED performance does not rest within the ED, but outside the departmental environs themselves. Although this may be a complex concept administratively, it is important to note the crucial importance of laboratory, radiology, and other ancillary services in the efficiency of the overall care process.

The cornerstone of the ED evaluation is often found in the laboratory itself, with the most common reason for delay being staff cutbacks. The scenario often involves an elimination or restriction of the phlebotomist's job role, in deference to the bedside nurse who now draws the blood concurrent with intravenous line (IV) placement. The downside of this approach is that the patient may get an unnecessary IV with its attendant co-morbidity. In addition to that, the effectiveness of the phlebotomist can often be significantly better than the harried nurse.

Solutions can include a blended program utilizing using both a phlebotomist for only the hardest cases and nursing for most others, allowing a decrease in laboratory staff on a hospital-wide basis. Most importantly, there may be a time for the physician to be introspective concerning the amount of testing required on the physician end and how it changes outcome. Fewer tests ordered means fewer blood draws and, ultimately, faster patient processing, resulting in a more efficient health care facility.

The radiology department is often confronted with delays as patient complexity increases, and the radiology technicians are overwhelmed as well. Another phenomenon is multitasking, where plain films are delayed for patients while the cross-trained technician performs computed tomography (CT) scans as well.

One constructive approach should include dedicated radiology and CT technicians, but this approach is often limited by budgetary constraints. The burden often shifts back to the ED physician to prescribe judicious use of available resources, often substituting a "more for less" available test. For example, CT resources are usually present and can be utilized with helical chest CT scanning to evaluate DVT when ultrasound resources may not be available.

Likewise, there may be issues regarding the ordering of multiple redundant studies of various body regions. There need be clear criteria for the use of x-rays, CT scans, MRIs for spinal injury, and CT and ultrasound for abdominal imaging. In some instances, a CT-only strategy can be utilized for cervical spine injury, while in others MRI may be added in select cases (Figure 12).

There is a particular problem with ultrasound technicians leaving hospital employ for office or imaging center-based jobs with no on-call requirement. Here, a helpful strategy uses an ultrasound (US protocol). This begins with pre-testing laboratory screening—such as a CBC, or LFTs for gallbladder ultrasound, D-dimer for DVT and quantitative beta hCG for pelvic ultrasound (Figure 13).

In addition, scheduling for next-day, first available, "urgent" ultrasound appointments is often an acceptable alternative for patients. This system works best with ED and radiology staff pre-registration and "first appointment of the daytime" slot, rather than having the patient himself call the next day.

Patient compliance with recommended medical regimens, such as follow-up with an outpatient physician from the ED, is particularly problematic, averaging less than one-third (27.8%) compliance in one study.[1] A subsequent interventional trial found that if specific personalized informative instructions are offered, compliance with discharge follow-up improves by one-third to 39.8% compliance.[2]

A significant improvement in patient compliance is achieved with a definitive appointment made for the patient with specific time and date of appearance. This manifests as a next-day radiology appointment form that is pre-formatted for next-day, first "urgent appointments" (Figure 14).

It should be noted that there is potential detriment to efficiency cost for every test ordered. The benchmark turn-around time (TAT) for a CBC is 30 minutes and 35–45 minutes for chest or extremity x-ray, and 90 minutes for CT scan.[3, 4] These benchmarks can be difficult to achieve in a busy, overwhelmed facility.

Figure 12. Cervical Spine Imaging Protocol

Cervical Spine Injury Protocol

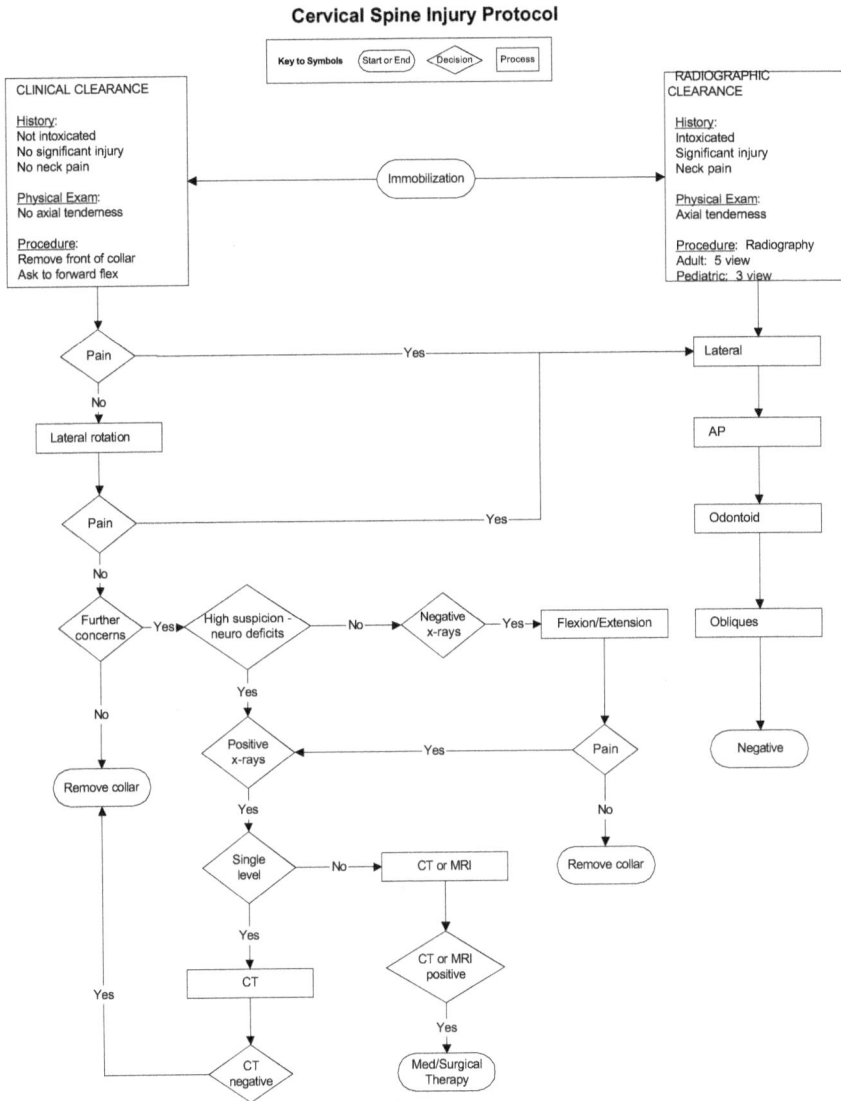

Key to Symbols (Start or End) ◁Decision▷ [Process]

CLINICAL CLEARANCE

History:
Not intoxicated
No significant injury
No neck pain

Physical Exam:
No axial tenderness

Procedure:
Remove front of collar
Ask to forward flex

RADIOGRAPHIC CLEARANCE

History:
Intoxicated
Significant injury
Neck pain

Physical Exam:
Axial tenderness

Procedure: Radiography
Adult: 5 view
Pediatric: 3 view

Immobilization

Pain — Yes — Lateral
No
Lateral rotation
Pain — Yes — AP
No
Odontoid
Further concerns — Yes — High suspicion - neuro deficits — No — Negative x-rays — Yes — Flexion/Extension — Obliques
No
Yes
Positive x-rays — Yes — Pain
Remove collar
Yes
Single level — No — CT or MRI
No — Negative
Remove collar
Yes
CT
CT or MRI positive
Yes
Yes
CT negative
Med/Surgical Therapy

Rade B. Vukmir, M.D., JD, FCCP, FACEP

This clinical guideline is part of our education, quality management, and risk management program, and has been prepared by ECI for its partners and affiliates. Information contained herein addresses emergency medical practice in general. It is not a substitute for the hospital's policies and procedures nor the practitioner's knowledge and skill in the care and treatment of any individual patient. This information may be utilized as a guide to assist in a wide variety of circumstances and is not intended to establish a standard of care.

Emergency Consultants, Inc. © 1999-2005

Revised December 21, 2004

Reference 5

Figure 13. Ultrasound Screening Protocol

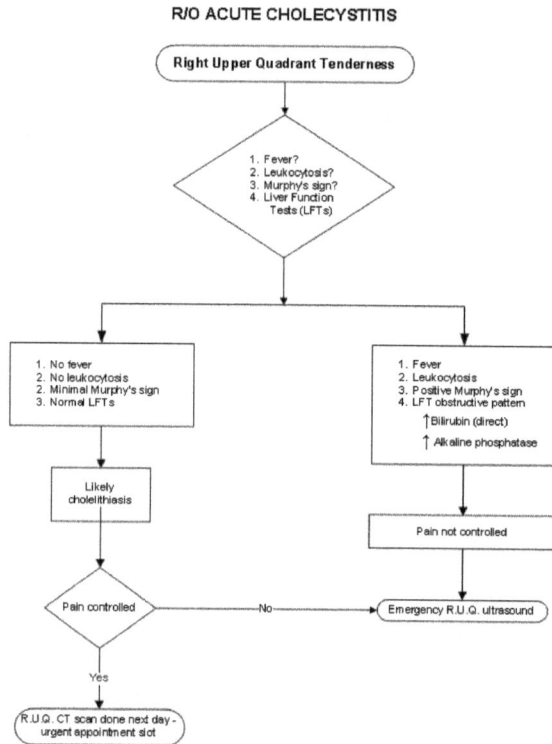

R/O ACUTE CHOLECYSTITIS

Right Upper Quadrant Tenderness

1. Fever?
2. Leukocytosis?
3. Murphy's sign?
4. Liver Function
   Tests (LFTs)

| 1. No fever 2. No leukocytosis 3. Minimal Murphy's sign 4. Normal LFTs | 1. Fever 2. Leukocytosis 3. Positive Murphy's sign 4. LFT obstructive pattern ↑ Bilirubin (direct) ↑ Alkaline phosphatase |

Likely cholelithiasis

Pain not controlled

Pain controlled ——No——→ Emergency R.U.Q. ultrasound

Yes

R.U.Q. CT scan done next day - urgent appointment slot

Reference 5

Figure 14. Radiology Next Day Appointment Form

Your Emergency Room physician has scheduled you for a test in the Vascular Lab for 8:40 AM, the morning of_____. Please arrive at the Vascular Lab, located on the second floor, at 8:00 AM. There will be NO need to check in at the business office.

_____You may eat/drink before this test.

_____You MAY NOT eat/drink before this test.

It is incumbent on the practicing emergency department physician (EDP) to both be a good steward of resources and to attempt to maximize efficiency. An ED benchmark is offered, referencing resources utilized in the patient evaluations, which include those who receive no labs or x-rays (29%), labs only (18%), x-rays only (13%) and both labs and x-rays (39%). Overall, one-third of patients receive no diagnostics while two-thirds receive some diagnostic intervention, having obvious adverse impact on efficiency[6] (Figure 15).

Figure 15. Resource Utilization Related to Turnaround Time (TAT)

Resources	Use (%)	TAT (Hr.)
None	33	1.2
X-ray	18	1.7
Lab	15	2.3
Lab/X-ray	34	2.8
Average	100	2.0

Reference 6

Ideally, the physician group should regress to the mean efficiency point with some providers augmenting and some restricting testing to optimize patient care and customer service.

Clearly, individualized hospitals' specific plans are necessary based on laboratory and radiology capability, patient needs, and radiologist diagnostic acumen. A cooperative approach balancing patient needs and convenience with both ED and radiology capability is necessary.

References

1. Vukmir, R.B., Kremen, R., Dehart, D.A., Menegazzi, J. "Compliance with emergency department patient referral." *American Journal of Emergency Medicine* 1992; 10(5): 413–7.

2. Vukmir, R.B., Kremen, R., Ellis, G.L., Dehart, D.A., Plewa, M.C., Menegazzi, J. "Compliance with emergency department referral: The effect of computerized discharge instructions." *Annals of Emergency Medicine* 1993; 22(5): 819–23.

3. "Benchmarking in Emergency Services." *ACEP Management Course Manual* 1994: 7.

4. *Benchmark ED Staffing Ratios Based on Facility Size.* VHA Database, 2001.

5. Emergency Consultants Inc.© Vukmir, R., O'Rourke, I. *QualChart Information Systems Patient Management Program.* Traverse City, MI. Revision 4.04; 2005–2006.

6. Emergency Consultants Inc.© "Group Utilization." *Vital Signs* 2006: B-4.

Chapter 6

Emergency Medicine Workforce

Contemporary estimates of ED workplace requirements have been offered periodically, analyzing available hospital ED positions and workforce.

In 1997, it was estimated that the need for full-time emergency physicians was 20–25,000 positions, with a range of anywhere from 15–30,000 ED jobs available. At that point in time, approximately one-half of the positions (13,000) were held by trained EM physicians, assuming an annual attrition rate of 3% and graduation rate of 900–1000 EM residents annually.[1]

They described a model where the current annual output of EM residents would balance a 30,000 emergency physician cohort if a 3% annual attrition rate was hypothesized, a 22,000 group if a 4% attrition but only a 15,000 ED physician group if 6% attrition was encountered. They projected that the output of EM residents would only equal demand in the year 2030. This approach does not factor in positions held by non-EM board-certified physicians performing these tasks.

The staffing proforma found that the average hospital ED had 4.96 full-time equivalent (FTE) EDPs per site working an average of 40 hours per week and 7.48 EDPs per site, factoring in part-time physicians (PTE) to the staffing mix.[2] The ratio of total to full-time physicians was 1.5:1, and the ratio of American Board of Emergency Medicine Certification was 48% in 1998.

Interestingly, most (90%) residency-trained or certified EDPs worked in multiple EDs, in their day-to-day practice. The staffing models employed by hospitals were varied. Physician employees were found in 44% of hospitals, where 49% were staffed by independent contractor physicians in this study. Currently, a similar ratio applies to management-group-based contracted physicians versus hospital employed physicians (60:40).

Mid-level providers are employed in increasing numbers as well. PAs are found in 29% of EDs, where 12% utilized nurse practitioners (NPs), and 6% employed both PA/NPs to supplement physician staffing or provide goal-directed integrated care.

Their overall projection in 1998 was that the emergency medicine workforce needed 37,000 physicians, assuming 7.5 physicians per facility (5.0 FTE/2.5 PTE) or 32,000 total physicians accounting for those working as multiple slots.

A follow-up study was published in 2002 noting first a 5% decline in the number of hospitals in operation from 5329 to 5064.[3] There were 7.85 total and 5.29 full-time physicians per institution on average. This physician group worked approximately 40 hours per week clinically as well.

A demographic profile of the EDP finds an average age of 42.6 years, where 83% were male, and 82% were caucasian. The training profile found practitioners were EM-trained in 42%, ABEM-certified in 50%, and certified in emergency medicine including non-ABEM "certification" pathways.

The trends noted included an increase in FTEs per institution from 5.11 to 5.35, but a 5% decline in number of hospitals overall. The staffing requirements suggested were 39,500 physicians if working a single site and 32,000 incorporating multiple-site-employed physicians.

Therefore, conclusions can be drawn concerning the ED provider work force. There are approximately 5000 hospitals and 4500 Emergency departments with 40% employee physicians and 60% subcontracted that service.[4] There are approximately 40,000 ED jobs nationally with about half certified in emergency medicine with EM training in 40%.

Currently, one half of ED's saw less than 20,000 visits annually.[4] A staffing model can be predicted by ED patients seen where 15,000 annual visits or less finds it difficult to support 5 EM physicians without a significant financial stipend. This size of a facility is often staffed with family practice providers or non-ABEM EM-certified EDPs.

On the other hand, a volume of 20 to 25,000 visits with adequate payor mixture should be able to support an EM-certified physician group. It is this middle ground with 15–20,000 annual visits that may require a modest "investment" or stipend to obtain proper emergency department staffing with EM-trained or certified physicians.

Another commonly asked question is, "When do I need a midlevel provider to assist in the ED operation?" The single physician model allows one to see approximately 17,500 patients annually, while a 2-physician model allows 26,300 patient visits. Common recommendations find that a midlevel provider is utilized in the model where between 18–22,000 ED visits are evaluated annually.

Certainly, these approaches and recommendations need be individualized to the specific location.

References

1. Holliman, C.J., Wuerz, R.C., Chapman, D.M., Hirshberg, A.J. "Workforce projections for emergency medicine: how many emergency physicians does the United States need?" *Acad Emergency Medicine* 1997; 4(7): 725–30.

2. Moorhead, J.C., Gallery, M.E., Manile, T., Chaney, W.C., Conrad, L.C., Dalsey, W.C., Herman, S., Hockberger, R.S., McDonald, S.C., Packard, D.C., Rapp, M.T., Rorrie, C.C. Jr., Schafermeyer, R.W., Schulman, R., Whitehead, D.C., Hirschkorn, C., Hogan, P. "A study of the workforce in emergency medicine." *Annals of Emergency Medicine* 1998; 31(5): 595–607.

3. Moorhead, J.C., Gallery, M.E., Hirshkorn, C., Barnaby, D.P., Barsan, W.G., Conrad, L.C., Dalsey, W.C., Fried, M., Herman, S.H., Hogan, P., Mannie, T.E., Packard, D.C., Perina, D.G., Pollack, C.V., Rapp, M.T., Rorrie, C.C., Schafermeyer, R.W. "A study of the workforce in emergency medicine: 1999." *Annals of Emergency Medicine* 2002; 40(1): 3–15.

4. Burt, C.W., McCaig, L.F. "Staffing, Capacity, and Ambulance Diversion in Emergency Departments: United States, 2003–04." *Advance Data From Vital and Health Statistics, U.S. Department of Health and Human Services* 2006; 376; September 27: 1–12.

Chapter 7

Physician Efficiency

There have been numerous factors affecting ED physician efficiency outside of the physician's individual level of expertise, proficiency, and work ethic. The three most obvious factors are the number and rapidity of patients presenting to the ED, accompanied by their acuity, often quantified as the admission rate.

The average number of recommended patient encounters in the ED is 2.0 patients per hour, with an evaluation range of 1.8–2.0 pph.[1] As the medical system comes under greater strain, this patient evaluation ratio has had a compelled increase to 2.1 (range of 1.9–2.3) and subsequently 2.2 (range of 2.0–2.4) patients per hour in some locations (Figure 16).

Figure 16. Physician Staffing Models

Average (pph)	Range
2.0	1.8 - 2.2
2.1	1.9 - 2.3
2.2	2.0 - 2.4
2.25	2.0 - 2.5

Volume-Based Physician Staffing Model

Average (pph)	ED Volume (annual patients)
1.96	< 20,000 small
2.05	20-30,000 modest
2.41	30-40,000 moderate
2.06	40-50,000 large

References 2, 3

In fact, there are some programs that anticipate practitioners evaluate 2.5 patients per hour under the auspices of a heavily incentivized compensation plan. The American Academy of Emergency Medicine (AAEM) mandates a 2.5 pph maximum guideline.[4] The difficulty with such a plan is that improved efficiency goals are offset by adverse medicolegal consequences, as well as adverse customer service tradeoffs.

Another staffing model incorporates the facility size in the recommendations for physician and midlevel staffing. There is an interesting non-linear distribution of work force associated with annual ED patients visits. Small facilities (< 20, 0000 annual visits) are staffed at 1.96 pph, modest facilities (20–30,000) at 2.05 pph, moderate facilities (30–40,000) at 2.41 pph and large facilities (40–50,000 visits) at 2.06 pph.[1, 3] The efficiency appears to peak in the moderate-sized facility with the least efficiency found in the smaller facilities.

It should be noted as well that there is a non-uniform distribution of patient presentation with approximately 0.5 patients per hour shifted from day to night shift, resulting in 2.5 patients per hour and 1.5 patients per hour evaluated respectively on the night and day shifts. Therefore, more aggressive staffing ratios can force the EDP to evaluate 3–3.5 patients per hour during some peak "daytime" periods. Although the EM practitioner is "expert" at seeing significant fluctuations in patient volume, this average, if sustained, extracts significant cost in efficiency and service orientation from the health care providers for patients.

The payor financial class mix can have significant impact on the ED operational efficiency as well. Currently, "self-pay" status combined with Medicaid as method of payment in a 40% or greater proportion is often associated with significant operational financial hardship. This presents dual dilemmas for ED with operational difficulties due to underfunding and significant "cost shifting" to "paying" patients who might endeavor to pay the bill for all patient services rendered. It is crucial to recognize that this is not an "ER" problem, but a "hospital problem," and until adequate funding can be provided by patients themselves, the state, or the federal government, the issue will persist. Until that endpoint can be achieved, the operating capital must be provided by the hospital as a stipend to adequately staff and motivate the physician staff.

However, rather than view the ED as a "cost center," you must recognize its significance as a "profit center." Remember, the ED serves as the admission portal for 50–75% of patients admitted to the hospital. Another significant financial contribution is made in the area of testing referral, where the laboratory and radiology departments, and indirectly, the hospital itself benefit from testing referrals. In fact, approximately 60–75% of patients receive either lab, x-ray or both services provided during the ED visit, establishing the opportunity for benefits accrued to these areas.

As emergency medicine is a relatively new specialty with board certification first achieved in 1976, it has morphed into a multi-generational specialty. Training programs have decreased on-call ratios from every other day to one in seven days today in some cases as resident work hours are restricted.

This phenomenon represents significant challenges as the baby boomers, generation Xrs, the 70s latchkey kids, or now the millennials—born in the 80s to 90s with significant parental involvement—or generation Y grads are working their way into the system. They appear to be technologically savvy and achievement-oriented, but tend to desire a less intense work schedule. The best mix, therefore, is a multigenerational staff model. Here, there is cross-pollination with more experienced staff offering guidance on staff relationships and work ethic, while less experienced personnel offer technological advancement and other new learning techniques to the older physicians.

The burgeoning malpractice crisis and its associated defensive medicine slow down has had a huge impact on ED efficiency. The "perfect storm" concept is in play and the EDP is required to see more patients, of higher complexity, with more stringent legal standards applied to medical malpractice associated with these encounters.

Several approaches to the problem have been suggested. First, "peer review" should indeed be expert review. ED cases should be reviewed by other ED physicians rather by than a hospital-based physician of another specialty since the care emphasis often differs. Instead, a critical care specialist who works in the ICU setting can be a good "peer" reviewer for emergency cases. Particularly contentious cases should be sent for external review to an unbiased outside observer to avoid further care debate.

Likewise, protocolization of care helps to avoid staff conflicts. Guidelines should be evidence-based, multidisciplinary in development, and reviewed every 2 years. These recommendations are best understood in an algorithmic form and should be formalized and approved in a patient care committee. Here, we offer clinical care protocols for non-ST segment elevation myocardial infarction (NSTEMI) (Figure 17) and community-acquired pneumonia (CAP) (Figure 18).

Figure 17. Chest Pain Protocol

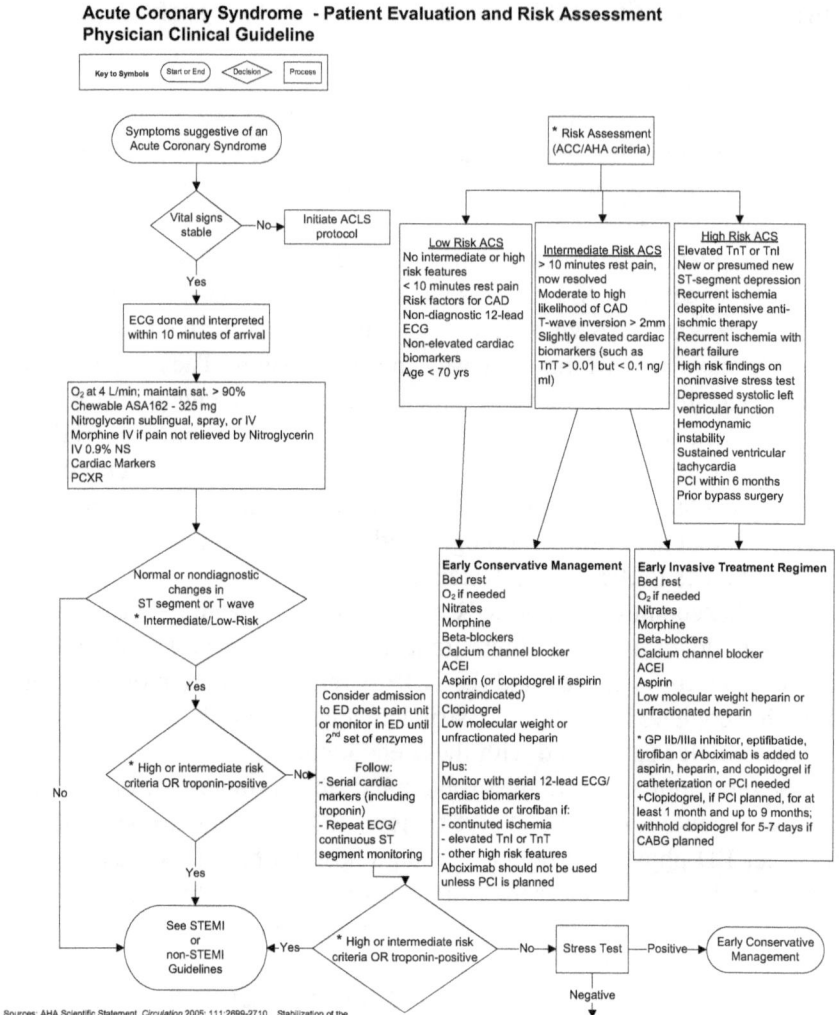

Acute Coronary Syndrome - Patient Evaluation and Risk Assessment Physician Clinical Guideline

Sources: AHA Scientific Statement. *Circulation* 2005; 111:2699-2710. Stabilization of the patient with acute coronary syndromes. *Circulation* 2005; 112:89-110.

This clinical guideline is part of our education, quality management, and risk management program, and has been prepared by ECI for its partners and affiliates. Information contained herein addresses emergency medical practice in general. It is not a substitute for the hospital's policies and procedures nor the practitioner's knowledge and skill in the care and treatment of any individual patient. This information may be utilized as a guide to assist in a wide variety of circumstances and is not intended to establish a standard of care.

Emergency Consultants, Inc.© 1999-2006

Revised April 2006

Reference 5

Figure 18. Pneumonia Protocol

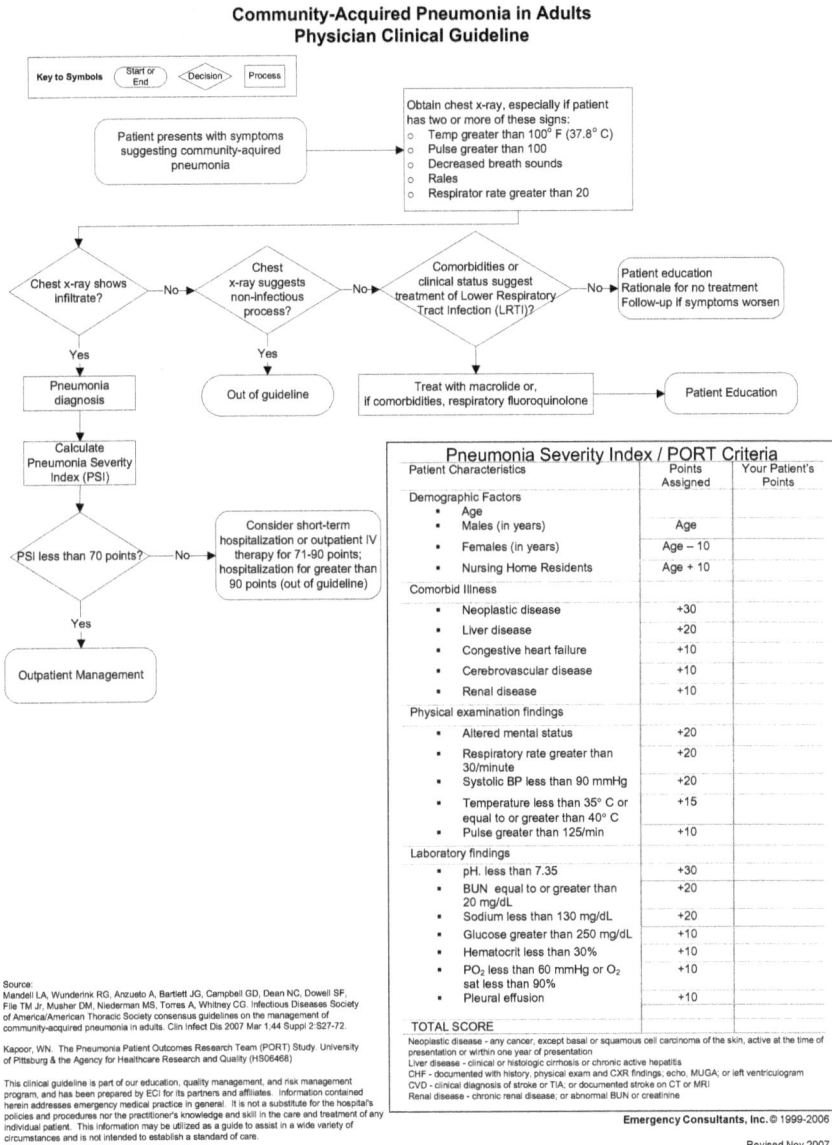

Community-Acquired Pneumonia in Adults
Physician Clinical Guideline

Key to Symbols — Start or End / Decision / Process

Patient presents with symptoms suggesting community-aquired pneumonia →

Obtain chest x-ray, especially if patient has two or more of these signs:
- Temp greater than 100° F (37.8° C)
- Pulse greater than 100
- Decreased breath sounds
- Rales
- Respirator rate greater than 20

Chest x-ray shows infiltrate? —No→ Chest x-ray suggests non-infectious process? —No→ Comorbidities or clinical status suggest treatment of Lower Respiratory Tract Infection (LRTI)? —No→ Patient education / Rationale for no treatment / Follow-up if symptoms worsen

Yes ↓

Pneumonia diagnosis

Yes ↓

Out of guideline

Treat with macrolide or, if comorbidities, respiratory fluoroquinolone → Patient Education

↓

Calculate Pneumonia Severity Index (PSI)

↓

PSI less than 70 points? —No→ Consider short-term hospitalization or outpatient IV therapy for 71-90 points; hospitalization for greater than 90 points (out of guideline)

Yes ↓

Outpatient Management

Pneumonia Severity Index / PORT Criteria

Patient Characteristics	Points Assigned	Your Patient's Points
Demographic Factors		
• Age		
• Males (in years)	Age	
• Females (in years)	Age – 10	
• Nursing Home Residents	Age + 10	
Comorbid Illness		
• Neoplastic disease	+30	
• Liver disease	+20	
• Congestive heart failure	+10	
• Cerebrovascular disease	+10	
• Renal disease	+10	
Physical examination findings		
• Altered mental status	+20	
• Respiratory rate greater than 30/minute	+20	
• Systolic BP less than 90 mmHg	+20	
• Temperature less than 35° C or equal to or greater than 40° C	+15	
• Pulse greater than 125/min	+10	
Laboratory findings		
• pH. less than 7.35	+30	
• BUN equal to or greater than 20 mg/dL	+20	
• Sodium less than 130 mg/dL	+20	
• Glucose greater than 250 mg/dL	+10	
• Hematocrit less than 30%	+10	
• PO$_2$ less than 60 mmHg or O$_2$ sat less than 90%	+10	
• Pleural effusion	+10	
TOTAL SCORE		

Neoplastic disease - any cancer, except basal or squamous cell carcinoma of the skin, active at the time of presentation or within one year of presentation
Liver disease - clinical or histologic cirrhosis or chronic active hepatitis
CHF - documented with history, physical exam and CXR findings; echo, MUGA; or left ventriculogram
CVD - clinical diagnosis of stroke or TIA; or documented stroke on CT or MRI
Renal disease - chronic renal disease; or abnormal BUN or creatinine

Source:
Mandell LA, Wunderink RG, Anzueto A, Bartlett JG, Campbell GD, Dean NC, Dowell SF, File TM Jr, Musher DM, Niederman MS, Torres A, Whitney CG. Infectious Diseases Society of America/American Thoracic Society consensus guidelines on the management of community-acquired pneumonia in adults. Clin Infect Dis 2007 Mar 1;44 Suppl 2:S27-72.

Kapoor, WN. The Pneumonia Patient Outcomes Research Team (PORT) Study. University of Pittsburg & the Agency for Healthcare Research and Quality (HS06468)

Emergency Consultants, Inc.© 1999-2006

Revised Nov 2007

Reference 5, 6

Another issue especially pertinent to the ED physician is the "burn-out" phenomenon, which can have associated adverse effects on both quality and quantity of patient care delivered. Although it is commonly felt that the problem is due to working nights, weekends, and holidays under very trying conditions, it is most likely not predominantly due to any of these factors at all.

The most likely factors associated with the ED burnout is the too-frequent negative feedback offered for performing a job function—which is usually in the patient's best interest. A common form of this interaction arises from a medical staff member, who is asked to admit a patient, and there is a difference of opinion about the necessity of the need for admission. Sometimes, a significant factor in the disagreement simply distills down to the physician's workload.

The ED patient population is often beset with a host of nonmedical conditions over which the ED staff have no control. This may result in an extraordinary number of care reimbursement denials, further exacerbating the medical staff–ED interface on the inpatient service.

Ideally, an optimally functioning emergency system has the ED physicians doing "their" job to the highest level of performance. Again, it is usually in the patient's and hospital's best interest to have this premise as the desired endpoint.

A standardized approach to the admission process—utilizing admission profiles commercially available, such as the InterQual® Admission Evaluation Criteria (McKesson Corp., San Francisco, CA) (Figure 19)—is generally useful. These profiles can be dove-tailed with case management analysis to generalize a standardized approach, with differences of opinion referred to the case management or patient care committee for analysis, decision, and education.

Clearly, referral to a case management-based patient care committee could assist the oft-encountered physician debate about who is to be admitted or discharged from the ED.

Figure 19. McKesson CareEnhance ® Review Manager 6.0

Product: LOC: Acute Adult
Subset: Cardiovascular / Peripheral Vascular (Acute)
Admission both:
　Severity of illness
　　(Onset within 1 wk)
　　　✓ **Severity of Illness, ≥ One**
　　　CLINICAL FINDINGS
　　　✓ Acute / Progressive tissue loss *and* known PVD
　　　DVT, **≥ one**:
　　　Dyspnea *and* hemodynamically stable (systolic BP **> 100), ≥ one:**
　　　Pericarditis, **≥ one**:
　　　Peripheral / Femoral pulse absent / decreased, ≥ one:
　　　Syncope / Presyncope, **≥ one**:
　　　IMAGING FINDINGS
　　　LABORATORY FINDINGS
　　　　Blood Gases
　　　　Chemistry
　Intensity of Service
　　(At Least Daily)
　　　Intensity of Service, ONE:

References

1. *American College of Emergency Physicians: Policy Statement.* ACEP 1994.

2. "Benchmarking in Emergency Services." *ACEP Management Course Manual* 1994: 7.

3. *Benchmark ED Staffing Ratios Based on Facility Size.* VHA Database, 2001.

4. *American Academy of Emergency Medicine: Emergency physician-to-patient ED staffing ratios.* AAEM Board of Directors February 22, 2001.

5. Emergency Consultants Inc.© Vukmir, R., O'Rourke, I. *QualChart Information Systems Patient Management Program.* Traverse City, MI. Revision 4.04; 2005–2006.

6. Fine, M.J., Auble, T.E., Yealy, D.M., Hanusa, B.H., Weissfeld, L.A., Singer, D.E., Coley, C.M., Marrie, T.J., Kapoor, W.N. "A Prediction Rule to Identify Low-Risk Patients with Community-Acquired Pneumonia." *New England Journal of Medicine* 1997; January 23; 336(4): 243–50.

Chapter 8

Mid-level (PA/NP) Provider Efficiency

The first studies of midlevel providers, which include physician assistants (PA) and nurse practitioners (NP), comparing quality of care were performed not long after the primary board certification of the emergency medicine discipline itself was achieved.

A meta-analysis of 45 studies comparing PA/NP to physician care was performed to report some interesting trends.[1] It found that in a significant proportion of studies, patients were at least as pleased, if not more pleased, with NP/PA than with physician provided care. Process variable analysis finds no difference in outcome between patients seen by midlevel providers compared to physicians.

The emergency nurse provider (ENP) is an RN with specific postgraduate training, who functions in conjunction with the supervision of a physician functioning in an expanded role in the ED setting. Patients responded to a questionnaire study to report that this care was prompt (78%), courteous (92%), received a good or satisfactory rating (90%), was thorough (92%) and most (94%) said they would be examined by a NP again.[2]

There was a subtle physician bias concerning disease complexity, where the physicians felt the NP performed adequately in 93% of non-urgent cases, 80% in urgent, but only 59% in emergent cases. Over time, the advent of critical care NP programs in addition to the primary care NP certification programs have effected a positive change in this area as well.

Since the first physician assistant graduates provided care in 1966, the advent of this service has served to increase the affordability of ED care.[3] It was suggested that 62% of all ED providers could be handled by a PA, with physician consultation required in 31% of the cases and only 7% that required direct physician intervention.[4]

There was a resounding endorsement of this profile as the majority (97%) of patients felt they could be seen again by the PA if the need should ever arise.

This is indeed a worldwide trend, with the British system embracing midlevel care as well. However, this survey found that only 9% of patients were managed primarily by the NP alone, with the majority (86%) of cases related to trauma, and not medical illness. The suitability of care protocols for this endeavor was documented as appropriate in most cases.[5]

Another important consideration is the beneficial effect on customer service. A study directly comparing care by NP to physician controls found equivalent overall satisfaction rates (3.9 vs. 4.0) on a 1 (poor) to 5 (excellent) linear scale.[6] Most patients (80%) were non-committal on a repeat visit assignment to a midlevel, while 10% would prefer to see a physician or midlevel exclusively.

The use of PAs in the ED has been largely successful as well, featured in 50% of EDs nationally. A recent survey found a high level of satisfaction (93%), not influenced by patient's age, gender, or insurance status.[7] Interestingly, most of patients (88%) indicated they would not be willing to wait longer to receive care from an EDP. Those willing to wait would only be delayed an additional 30 minutes for physician care.

The advantages of a midlevel provider in the ED setting include benefits on efficiency and customer service, with an associated positive financial impact. PA/NP providers are capable of evaluating and meeting a wide variety of medical and surgical conditions in the ED setting. There is a large proportion of patients that prefer the "kinder and gentler" care of the midlevel provider. Lastly, the financial benefits offer a greater proportion of potential ED patients' access to care. As patient care reimbursement progressively declines and unfunded mandates exist to care for additional ED patients, it becomes mandatory to include these numbers in your staffing plan. Antiquated staffing models suggest midlevels can see patients in a 0.5–0.75: 1 ratio with physicians, resulting in 1.0–1.5 pph rate.

Currently, midlevels are capable of seeing 2.5 (2.0–3.0) pph, which at today's reduced reimbursement rates may be required to allow the program to survive, while an exclusively physician-staffed model requires an extensive subsidy to see the same patient volume.

There is a balance, however, requiring direct physician supervision of mid-levels to care for the more critically ill or admitted patients.

References

1. Sox, H.C., Jr. "Quality of patient care by nurse practitioners and physician's assistants: a ten-year prospective." *Annals of Internal Medicine* 1979; 91(3): 459–68.

2. Alongi, S., Geolot, D., Richter, L., Mapstone, S., Edgerton, M.T., Edlich, R.F. "Physician and patient acceptance of emergency nurse practitioners." *Journal of the American College of Emergency Physicians* 1979; 8(9): 357–9.

3. Friedman, M.M. "A physician's assistant in your ED?" *Emergency Medical Services* 1979; 8(3): 68.

4. Maxfield, R.G., Lemire, M.D., Thomas, M., Wansleben, O.; "Utilization of supervised physician's assistants in emergency room coverage in a small rural community hospital." *Journal of Trauma* 1975; 15(9): 795–9.

5. Read, S.M., Jones, N.M., Williams, B.T. "Nurse practitioners in accident and emergency departments: what do they do?" *British Medical Journal*, 1992; 305(6867): 1466–1470.

6. Rhee, K.J., Dermyer, A.L. "Patient satisfaction with a nurse practitioner in a University Emergency Service." *Annals of Emergency Medicine* 1995; 26(2): 130–2.

7. Counselman, F.L., Graffeo, C.A., Hill, J.T. "Patient satisfaction with physician assistants (PAs) in an ED fast track." *American Journal of Emergency Medicine* 2000; 18(6): 661–5.

Chapter 9

Nursing Efficiency

E D overcrowding is as much related to lack of bed availability due to nursing staff shortages as any other factor, both within the ED proper and the hospital wards. There are objective nursing staffing ratios utilized, as well as those for physicians. The nursing staff ratio is measured as hours of care delivered per patient (hppv), which is the converse of the physician strategy, defined as patients seen per hour (pph) (Figure 20). The nurses are expected to provide 2.26 average (range of 0.6–4.6) hours of care per patient.[1] This approach can be at times difficult to understand and associated with much greater variability than the physician staffing model.[2, 3, 4] However, the AAEM suggests a 1.25–1.30 nursing pph staffing ratio.[5]

Figure 20. ED Staffing Estimates

$$\text{Nursing}$$

$$\text{hppv} = \frac{\text{paid nursing hours}}{\text{number of patients}}$$

$$\text{Physician}$$

$$\text{pph} = \frac{\text{number of patients}}{\text{paid physician hours}}$$

Another modification of this staffing model incorporates the facility volume in nursing service (RN/technician/clerical staff) hours worked per unit. ED visits in the small facilities ($< 24{,}000$) require 2.16 hppv, moderate facilities (24–48,000) require 2.37 hppv, and large facilities (48–72,000) require a 2.66 hppv staffing ratio[2] (Figure 21).

Figure 21. Nursing Service Efficiency Based on Patient Volume

Facility	Annual ED Visits	HPPV (hr/visit)
Small	< 24,000	2.16
Moderate	24-48,000	2.37
Large	48-72,000	2.66

HPPV = Nursing Source (RN/Tech/Clerical) hours worked per patient visit.

Reference 2

Unlike physician staffing, nursing staffing sometimes becomes less efficient as the facility size increases. This may be due to the increasing complexity of the patient mix encountered in larger facilities.

The simplest approach is to utilize the nurse-to-patient ratio of 1 nurse to 4.5 (range of 3.0-6.0) patients in the ED.[6, 7] The lower end of the range is activated with more critically ill patients cared for. Typical recommendations include a 1:1 ratio for trauma, 1:2 for critical care, and a 1:4 ratio for ED patients[8, 9] (Figure 22). However, some facilities utilize a 1:6 ratio in non-peak times, usually in the early morning hours (12 am–6 am).

Figure 22. Nurse-to-Patient Staffing Ratio

Hospital Unit	Nurse: Patient Ratio
Operating Room	1:1
Trauma Emergency Unit	
Critical/Intensive Care Unit	1:2
Labor/Delivery	
Emergency Department	1:3-4
Medical-Surgical Unit	1:4-6
Rehabilitation Unit	1:5

Reference 6, 7, 8, 9

In fact, some states—California being the first—have certified these recommendations through their respective health departments.[7] Other states have also mandated that no fewer than two nurses can be present in the ED at any one time to ensure the safety of ED operations.[9]

Further refinement of these observations from a 120-hospital cohort—classified as community hospitals (51%), teaching hospitals (38%), and rural hospitals (11%)—found that the largest proportion of sites was in the 2.5–3.1 hppv staffing range, with the mid-range group at 2.3–3.0 for nursing personnel. The indirect hppv was 0.5 (0.8–1.1) and there was a mid-range of 0–1.9 for non-nursing personnel.[10] Inter-institutional comparisons found that the most nursing resources were provided in teaching hospitals (3.0), followed by community hospitals (2.7) and finally rural hospitals (2.4) hppv.

The latest comparison utilized a 1.94 worked hours per visit and 2.09 hppv if nonproductive time is incorporated, as an Emergency Department average.[10]

However, it is crucial to recognize that the preeminent ED nursing organization—the Emergency Nurses Association (ENA)—does not accept staffing ratios, nor does it accept productivity output ratios as discussed.[3] The ENA position statement suggests that it "opposes mandated staffing ratios or other unilateral methods for determining nurse staffing in the ED." Best practice staffing must account for six key variables, as well as the sheer number of patients encountered[3, 4] (Figure 23). This organization thinks that these approaches fail to account for variation in patient acuity, length of stay, and individual staff capability, but can be modified by an inpatient care intensity rating[3, 11] (Figure 24).

Figure 23. ENA Staffing Guidelines

Six Key Variables
1. Census
2. Acuity
3. Length of stay
4. Nursing time for interventions and activities
5. Factoring in patient acuity
6. Skill mix
    Delegation of nursing interventions to non-RN personnel
7. Adjustment factor
    Non-patient care time (meetings, education)

Reference 4

Figure 24. Inpatient Intensity Rating

Level 1: Minimal Intensity
   a. Nurse / subject ratio 1:3 or 1:4
   b. No data/specimen collection or collected only once
   c. Subject healthy volunteer
   d. Independent with ADLs

Level 2: Minor Intensity
   a. Nurse / subject ratio 1:2 or 1:3
   b. Data/specimen collection less than every 2 hours
   c. Subject with minor dependent needs
   d. Some health maintenance support required
   e. Periodic monitoring more than every 2 hours

Level 3: Moderate Intensity
   a. Nurse / subject ratio 1.1 or 1:2
   b. Data specimen collection every 1-2 hours
   c. Subject moderately dependent; requires some assistance with Activities of Daily Living (ADLs), or assistance with discharge planning
   d. All pediatric patients

Level 4: High Intensity
Requires intensive PK blood sampling, titrating IV meds, multiple IV pumps, or studies requiring every hour nursing intervention
   a. Nurse / subject ratio 1:1
   b. Data/specimen collection at 1 min–1 hour intervals
   c. Subject totally dependent
   d. Intensive assistance required
   e. IV infusion of investigational drugs, immunotherapy or vaccines

Reference 4

   The newest approach quantifies nursing functional output as nursing hours per patient per day. This output utilizes a combination of Registered Nurses (RNs), Licensed Practical Nurses (LPNs), and Certified Nurse's Aides (CNAs). The Iowa Intervention Project recommended a mix of 86.1% RN and 13.9% non-RN staff to be involved in the patient care event.[12]

Currently, the most common method is to calculate the "hours per patient visit" or HPPV. The HPPV is the number of nursing hours divided by the number of ED visits. The ENA cited this approach as problematic for failing to differentiate the acuity and complexity of the patient mix. They discuss an inpatient intensity rating (1-4) blending staffing ratio and the work product required.[12] The basic ratio is 1.0–5.0 hours per patient volume per day, ranging from maximal to least efficient with most facilities performing in the 2.0–4.0 range.[3, 12]

The ENA offers a computer-based staffing tool incorporating six factors—patient census, acuity, length of stay, nursing time, skill mix, and the incorporation of nonpatient care time such as break time or education.[4] They also offer a "minimum staffing" model for the 24-hour-a-day "smallest" ED operation to include 11 RN FTEs and 2 nonpatient care FTEs, for a total of 13.0 FTEs.[4]

A random analysis of an ENA testing sample of 10 ED sites was offered. The volume ranges from 12,000 to 64,000 annual visits with hours of coverage per patient from 1.82–4.69 with an average of 3.2 hours/patient/day in 2004.[4]

The interesting paradox is that decreased staffing is associated with worsened patient outcome, poor job satisfaction, and prolonged length of stay as hours of nursing coverage decrease.[11, 13]

The definitive study in the master was performed by Needleman, who found an association between hospital staffing by nurses and select adverse patient outcomes.[14] They found a total of 11.4 hours of nursing care provided per day with RNs providing two thirds of the care and LPNs/aides providing one third of the care. There was a direct correlation between an increase in RN hours from the 25th to the 75th percentile, which was associated with a 2.5% decrease in length of hospital stay and a 2.9% reduction in various morbidities, such as development of UTIs and GI bleed.

Understanding the dichotomous nature of the physician and nursing ED staffing models, the physician groups have embraced staffing ratios expressed as patients seen per hour per physician (pph) to some degree, while nursing has not endorsed staffing ratios represented as hours of care per patient per day (hppv), suggesting subtleties of patient complexity overwhelm simple numerical relationships.

The factor most widely associated with staff shortages, high turnover and poor employee morale is the perceived lack of support for those in the trenches; this is predictably followed by worsened patient satisfaction. In fact, there is often a paradoxical effect offered by sophisticated educational and career advancement programs. These ladder educational progression programs may accentuate the perceived difference between the caregivers and leaders.

References

1. Cavorous, C.A., Suby, C. "Results of the 2004 Annual survey of hours: Part 1." *Journal of Clinical Systems Management* 2005; 7–11.

2. *Benchmark ED Staffing Ratios Based on Facility Size*. VHA Database, 2001.

3. ENA, *Staffing in the emergency department: An issue brief for ENA members*. Des Plaines, Illinois. October 4, 2004; 1–4.

4. Ray, C.E., Jagim, M., Agnew, J., McKay, J.I., Sheehy, S. "ENA's new guidelines for determining emergency department nurse staffing." *Journal of Emergency Nursing* 2003; 29(3): 245–253.

5. *American Academy of Emergency Medicine: Emergency nurse-to-patient ED staffing ratios*. AAEM Board of Directors. February 22, 2001.

6. Landro, L. "Why Quota for Nurses Isn't Cure-All." The Informed Patient. *Wall Street Journal*. Dec. 13, 2006.

7. *Minimum Nurse Staffing Recommendations*. California AB 394. January 1, 2001.

8. Wilson, M.E., Howard, P.K. "ENA Letter to State Leader for Referencing Nursing Staffing Ratios." Dec. 10, 2004.

9. Nursing Staffing Standards for Patient Safety and Quality Care Act of 2005 (H.R. 1222).

10. Zimmerman, P.G. "Managers Forum: Hours per patient visit." *Journal of Emergency Nursing* 2006; 32(1): 84.

11. Stanton, M.W. "Research in action." *Hospital Nurse Staffing and Quality of Care* 2004; 14: 1–11.

12. Iowa Intervention Project, "Determining Cost of Nursing Interventions: A Beginning." *Nursing Economics* 2004; 19: 146–60.

13. Cho, S.H., Ketefian, S., Barkauskas, V.H. "The effects of nurse staffing on adverse outcomes, morbidity, mortality, and medical costs." *Nursing Research* 2003; 52(2): 71–9.

14. Needleman, J., Buerhaus, P., Mattke, S., Stewart, M., Zelevinsky, K. "Nurse-staffing levels and the quality of care in hospitals." *New England Journal of Medicine* 2002; 346(22): 1715–22.

Chapter 10

Ancillary Care Providers— Paramedics, Technicians, Unit Secretaries

The optimum approach is the shared responsibility and accountability of every employee, who have the power to make the daily operations succeed or fail. Empowered and motivated employees who feel their opinions and contributions matter are the core of this program.

Cross-training programs for health care professionals have proliferated, but they have been associated with mixed results. The two most common formats are the unit secretary–patient care technician and the housekeeping–patient care management hybrid job roles.

The major issue appears to be deficits in individual, specific accountability. Interestingly, programs that have returned to individual job assignments have prospered, improving both staff morale and customer service. These positions stress individual areas of responsibility improved by specific self-governance programs.

An effective use of the "Team Approach" model is the staff progression model of development. This requires at first a division of labor that identifies particular contributions to the work product by the unit secretary, technician, paramedic, LPN, RN, and RN specialist.

The use of ED technicians has been well- described with the group featuring military medic or EMT–paramedic training. Their skill set involves procedural assistance with lacerations, wound care, abscess drainage, orthopedic splinting, IV placement, and blood draws for laboratory assessment. They do not, however, administer medicine, interpret tests, answer EMS radio calls or function without physician supervision in most areas. The experience at the University of New Mexico found only 3 complaints with 450,000 visits over a 15-year period.[1]

Paramedics have also been utilized in the ED since the early 80's in about 20% of facilities nationally. The services they offered included general assistance (94%), patient transport (89%), IV access (78%), laboratory specimen transport (67%), medication administration (22%), laceration repair (11%), narcotic administration (11%), and endotracheal intubation (6%).[2]

Advantages of including a paramedic in the ED staffing model include improvement in the ED–EMS interface (100%), cost effectiveness (89%), and introduction of the prehospital perspective to the ED; while disadvantages include the introduction of intra-staff conflict (28%) and inadequate training (11%).

Overall, there was an economic benefit suggested with an hourly pay rate of 67% compared to that offered to the RN nursing staff. There was, however, an equal split in response to this staffing resource with the clinical aggressiveness of the group viewed as both a potential advantage and disadvantage, at least in a pediatric emergency medicine setting.

An effective use of the "Team Approach" model is the internal staff progression model of development. This requires at first a division of labor that identifies particular contributions to the effort, whether unit secretary, technician, paramedic, LPN, RN, or RN specialist.

The technician role is a great case in point, where the basic job description can be modified to a two-level position involving transport, EKG performance, and patient assistance, to include specimen collection, IV starts, and patient monitoring during off-unit testing (Figure 24).

Here, the chance for advancement within the job category or grade is a tremendous motivator of staff performance. This same model works for the clerical-registration or unit secretary position as well. These positions also have good familiarity with the medical and patient care operation of the unit, allowing progression of job classification within the various job roles.

This advancement is formalized as a self-cultivated RN educational program where both technicians and clerical staff undergo nursing education and training. They are a natural for the transition with educational funds owed a forbearance for a facility employment, usually on a year-to-year basis.

Figure 24. ED Technician Job Description

EMERGENCY SERVICES TECHNICIAN DUTIES
The main duty of the ER Technician is to keep the patients moving.

To be done daily:
- Check O_2 tanks in each exam room, triage, and crash carts (check log).
- Check linen in each room (check log).
- Check supplies in each room including putting supplies & sterile returns away (check log).
- Check the refrigerator temperatures daily: two in the med room, one in patient pantry, and one in the staff lounge (check log).
- Advise the appropriate personnel of any supplies that need to be ordered.
- Coverage for the Health Unit Coordinators during breaks.

Additional duties done as needed:
- Change needle boxes
- Stock blanket warmer
- Insert foley caths
- Make beds
- Deliver patients to rooms
- Deliver patients for Imaging Services studies
- Assist nursing staff as needed
- Assist the physicians as needed
- Help patients with use of bed pan and potty chair
- Collect urine specimens/I&O
- Crutch training
- Splint application under supervision of physician or nurse and only undisplaced fractures.
- Dressing change and application
- Set up suture trays or instruments for procedures
- Hold patients as needed (blood draws, LPs, sutures, psych)
- Assist with codes
- EKGs
- Blood draws
- Protect sterile field
- CPR during code situations

Be sure to carry the phone provided while working.
You will learn something new everyday.

The "Team Approach" should figure prominently in the operations program of the best emergency departments. The program begins internally, with all ED providers contributing in a positive way to improve the quality of patient care. This concept extends to other departments, as the ED can often drive efficiency of related units such as telemetry and intensive care units (ICU).

Remember, the ED is usually the epicenter of the hospital admissions process, often with 50–75% of patients admitted through the ED proper. For this reason, it is crucial that the entire hospital to recognize this team concept. The hospital admission wards and ED have the same staffing and efficiency problems as well, but the ED must retain the flex capacity to actually deal with the "true emergencies," as well as minor inconveniences.

Instead of the "Push Approach," where patients need be "forced" on the floor staff, a more useful paradigm would be the "Pull Approach," where the floor staff strives to fill the available beds with waiting patients. This approach is established by a well-designed incentive program to reward proactive admission behavior on the part of the floor nursing staff.

My suggested approach, the "Flex Admission Program," utilizes an admission nurse who is allowed to flex down when the work is complete when her patient cohort is admitted. The "admission" part of the admission process is often most work-intensive while the back-end care responsibilities may be less. This division of responsibility is attractive to different providers. Some providers, therefore, like the nature of the high-intensity admission process, knowing full well that they can leave the shift early. Others like the more routine maintenance care and would be willing to stay for the pre-established shift length with a lower intensity work requirement.

This "Flex" model may utilize two 1:6 (nurse:patient) care FTEs. The admission nurse can process 4–5 admissions and then depart, while the maintenance nurse may provide custodial care to 7–8 patients at a more leisurely pace. This approach uses the same resources and financial expenditure to care for the same patients, but also improves employee satisfaction.

The potential to create staff division and discord is to foster an environment where administrative personnel are not encouraged to perform clinical activities when needed. It is crucial that supervisory staff maintain their clinical skills. This periodic patient care contact allows one to maintain clinical skills, staff appreciation, and respect. This allows one to manage clinical and administrative dilemmas "down" as well as "up" effectively.

References

1. Sklar, D.P., Herring, M., Roth, P.B., Besante, R. "Emergency department technicians in a university-county hospital: a 15-year experience." *Annals of Emergency Medicine* 1989; 18(4): 401–5.

2. Zempsky, W.T., Haskell, G. "Paramedics as allied health care providers in the pediatric emergency department." *Pediatric Emergency Care* 1998; 14(5): 329–31.

Chapter 11

Data Processing

It is inherently obvious that the patient information such as previous visit history, laboratory data, and prior EKG should be readily available to the practitioners. However, many current formats use multiple data silos—not integrated repositories—requiring multiple separate passwords and access steps inhibiting efficiency.

When the patient goes through the registration process, the patient's information should be actively provided to the department via a secure data terminal that includes past visits and discharge. A more modest program can begin at least with retrieving the most recent EKG when a new one is performed, as well as the old medical records present at the facility.

There has been a great deal of excitement concerning physician order entry. However, detractors suggest this is another efficiency workaround, enlisting the highest paid personnel to perform clerical activity. This shifts responsibility to another cost center—from nursing to the physician area—while the unit secretary is shifted to patient care responsibilities associated with a nursing budget seeking cost savings in that area.

While proponents suggest this approach was adopted to decrease medical error and more recent evaluations; however, some have reported no improvement at all or, in fact, worsening of medication and administration errors.

Medication errors are a major concern. A prospective pediatric trial of computerized physician order entry (CPOE) examined adverse drug events (ADE) that were then separated into two subcategories: medication prescription errors (MPE) and rule violations (RV).[1]

The results were favorable with a decrease in ADE to 40.9% (2.2 to 1.3) RV from 97.9% (6.8 to 0.1) and MPEs from 99.4% (30.1 to 0.2) per 100 errors from an overall error reduction rate of 95.9%. It is important to note the greatest effect in so-called "writing" errors, and less so with adverse drug effects with potential patient harm.

Another trial of CPOE in a critically ill patient cohort found a significant increase in mortality from 2.8 to 6.6% after implementation.[2] The inference is that while physicians perform data entry tasks, more time-sensitive patient care therapy may be omitted.

A prophetic review entitled "Computerized Physician Order Entry: Helpful or Harmful?" suggested the apparent dichotomy of results.[3] They suggest that the process variables associated with CPOE have been improved, but the change in patient outcome is lacking. They also document a significant increase in costs and a potential for a parabolic increase in ADEs during the implementation phase. The optimum scenario for physician/secretary communication is to have dedicated data entry personnel with physician on-line clarification ability.

Another impediment to care involves the ever-burgeoning documentation requirements which involve multiple patient-focused but non-integrated items mandated by both external (JCAHO) or internal sources (hospital information dashboard).

One approach is to establish a centralized committee to oversee all documentation requirements to ensure feasibility, efficiency, and lack of redundancy. It is essential to ensure a properly functioning electronic interface and not hand-written documentation as the electronic data processing program—the Electronic Medical Record (EMR) is being developed.

A common problem is that data processing tasks begin with system capability and are not necessarily task specific. Ideally, data processing system development should begin with the end-user needs as a basis of operation.

Therefore, assessment of data capability and needs should begin with clinical staff and then 'constructed' by the information systems (IS) afterward for best use.

References

1. Potts, A.L., Barr, F.E., Gregory, D.F., Wright, L., Patel, N.R. "Computerized physician order entry and medication errors in a pediatric critical care unit." *Pediatrics* 2004; 113(1 Pt 1): 59–63.

2. Han, Y.Y., Carcillo, J.A., Venkataraman, T.S., Clark, R.S., Watson, R.C., Nguyen, T.C., Bayir, H., Orr, R.A. "Unexpected increased mortality after implementation of a commercially sold computerized physician order entry system." *Pediatrics* 2005; 116(6): 1506–1512.

3. Berger, R.G., Kichak, J.P. "Computerized physician order entry: helpful or harmful?" *Journal of the American Medical Informatics Association* 2004; 11(2): 100–103.

Chapter 12

Physical Plant: Space and Efficiency

As the healthcare system may be unable to provide adequate routine patient care options, the ED becomes overburdened. The lack of bed availability in some areas is indeed critical. The average ED should have one ED bedspace for approximately every 2000 patients of the visits evaluated.[1] In some facilities, there is no ability to increase the available treatment area. This leaves maximizing efficiency as the only viable option to evaluate additional patients.

The basis of this approach calls for standardization of patient care protocols. These protocols begin with the ability of triage and bedside nurses to start the test-ordering process at the outset of the care event. Here, we feature the asthma and chest pain nursing assessment protocols (Figures 25 and 26). These protocols focus on the time-consuming parts of the care chain such as urine, pregnancy test, or radiology testing procedures.

Lastly, this same standardization requirement extends to the physicians. They should adopt a panel testing approach to avoid unnecessary individual variation in the testing process, as well to avoid sequential testing or subsequent contingency testing based on earlier testing results that can significantly decrease the efficiency of the department. Likewise, it is prudent to evaluate the patient's needs for emergent ED versus outpatient referral testing.

This invokes the age-old "art of medicine" argument where somehow the doctor's decision-making process is irreparably harmed if individual variation is decreased. This clearly is not the case, as many variations in care can be accomplished. No one is compelled to do anything

Figure 25. Nursing Triage Protocols

EMERGENCY DEPARTMENT
NURSING ASSESSMENT AND TREATMENT GUIDELINES

ASTHMA

Nursing Assessment (Perform and Document):

Subjective: History of present illness
            Onset / duration / severity
            Associated symptoms: cough (productive?); sputum color; hemoptysis, fever
            Pain assessment (PQRST*)
            Interventions prior to arrival and response
        Past medical history: asthma, frequent URIs, environmental allergies
        Past surgical history
        Medications (prescription, OTC and herbal)
        Allergies
        LMP and reproductive history on all females after menarche
        Smoking history

Objective: Vital signs with pulse oximetry
        Pulse oximetry - notify physician if less than 95% on room air
        Height/weight (may use estimates provided by patient)
        Assess breath sounds, chest excursion, accessory muscle use, retractions
        Note any nasal flaring, stridor, drooling, grunting, inability to speak more than a few words
        Assess skin color, moisture, temperature

Treatment Guidelines:
    1. Assess ABCs
    2. Support airway as needed: nasal trumpet, oral airway, intubation
    3. Apply O_2 if indicated to maintain pulse oximetry over 90%
    4. Albuterol 0.5 ml + 2.5 ml 0.9% NS SVN may repeat x 3
    5. Peak flow monitoring before and after treatment and *record*
    6. If severe anticipate administration of
        Methylprednisolone 125 mg IV
        Magnesium Sulfate 2 gm IV over 20 minutes
    7. Epinephrine (1:1000) 0.3 ml subcutaneously if unable to comply with inhaler and
        severity dictates

Lab	**X-ray**	**ECG**	**Other**
None	None	Only if suspected pneumonia	Pulse oximetry Peak flow monitoring

---

*****PQRST** = **P** *(Provoking factors);* **Q** *(Quality);* **R** *(Region/Radiation);* **S** *(Severity);* **T** *(Time: onset/duration)*

Emergency Consultants, Inc. © 1999-2006
Revised 5/04

Reference 2

Figure 26. Chest Pain Protocol

==
EMERGENCY DEPARTMENT
NURSING ASSESSMENT AND TREATMENT GUIDELINES
==

CHEST PAIN

<u>Nursing Assessment (Perform and Document):</u>

Subjective: History of present illness
  Pain assessment (PQRST*)
  Associated symptoms: SOB, diaphoresis, nausea, vomiting, temp, cough (productive?)
  Interventions prior to arrival and response: rest, NTG, home O_2
 Past medical history: angina, MI, family hx, diabetes, risk factors
 Past surgical history
 Medications (prescription, OTC and herbal)
 Allergies
 LMP and reproductive history on all females after menarche
 Smoking history

Objective: Assess ABCs
 Vital signs
 Height/weight (may use estimates provided by patient)
 Skin assessment: color, temp, moisture
 Breath sounds
 Heart sounds

Treatment Guidelines:
  1. Start IV 0.9% NS TKO or saline lock (draw blood for labs when starting)
  2. O_2 @ 2 L - 4 L per nasal cannula
  3. Apply cardiac monitor
  4. Continuous pulse oximetry
  5. EKG - take to physician for reading within 10 minutes of arrival
  6. ASA 162 mg - 325 mg chewed
  7. Portable CXR
  8. Anticipate NTG, heparin, thrombolytics, analgesics, beta blockers

<u>Lab</u>	<u>X-ray</u>	<u>ECG</u>	<u>Other</u>
CBC	Portable CXR	Yes - take to	Continuous pulse ox
Cardiac panel or		physician for	ABGs (if pulse ox below
CK, CKMB, Troponin I,		interpretation	90% on room air
Basic metabolic panel,		within 10 min.	
PT / PTT		of arrival	
Drug levels			
Digoxin, etc.			
Myoglobin			
BNP - if possible CHF			

*$PQRST$ = P *(Provoking/palliative factors); Q (Quality); R (Region/Radiation); S (Severity); T (Time: onset/duration)*

Information contained herein addresses emergency medical practice in general, and is not a substitute for the physician's judgment, knowledge and skill in the care of any individual patient. This information may be utilized as a guide to assist the nurse in a wide variety of circumstances and is not intended to establish a standard of care.

Emergency Consultants, Inc.© 1999-2006
Revised 5/04

Reference 2

based on a test result. This process is clearly best suited to a high-risk condition such as chest pain where the medicolegal burden to perform "available" testing is well-established. The perception that a test that was readily available to the ED staff that was performed for the patient raises significant responsibility questions and in some cases even suggestion of punitive withholding associated with alleged aggravated negligence.

Likewise, early admission decision-making can rapidly improve turn-around time. This approach is also well-adapted to chest pain where the admission decision is made almost literally from the start of the care event. Here, most patients at moderate or high pre-morbid risk warrant admission independent of subsequent lab testing results.

If you were to ask the average ED practitioner—either the physician or nurse—you would be assured that bed boarding is their greatest problem affecting day-to-day operations. There can be a decrease in departmental efficiency of 30–50% on an average bed boarding day. The cost estimate of lost revenue per ED bedspace in 2006 averaged $400–$500 per hour and was only exceeded by the time for operating room space, at $600–$1000 per hour or, comparably, ICU bedspace at $5000–$8000 per day.

The "bed restriction" process begins with the lack of physical bedspace assignments, but actually boils down to "no nurses at all" or "no nurses able" to take additional patients at that point in time. As the medical ward processes its budget of wage costs, this "ED hold status" then converts the ED from a potential direct and indirect profit center into a cost center, causing the hospital to lose its new patient evaluation productivity capacity.

As discussed previously, it is crucial that the ward nurse can be incentivized, or at least *not disincentivized* to both accept new patients as well as expedite the discharge of current patients. Clearly, current programs may have little incentive to admit new or discharge old patients; in fact, they may disincentivize, suggesting that hard work is only rewarded with additional work. Again, one approach offered involves having a separate admission nurse who receives some indirect per-capita financial incentive through flex-time capability where early shift completion can be achieved. This would ensure that more admissions could be processed by this same staff.

Another area of focus is "Resource-Matching." Remember, in the patients' minds, all of their health care concerns may be "emergencies." It is difficult for them to acknowledge that their urgent or even routine visit—that could be evaluated in the office or clinic—is not a true emergency. Certainly, that is not their perception during their visit. Here, the goal is to try to match the provider with the patient care requirements for the patient presenting. The best approach in these circumstances utilizes a well-run minor emergency operation.

The terminology is an integral part of the program's success. The descriptive terms utilized include *fast track* or *rapid treatment* center—implying improved turnaround time. *Urgent care* center implies less than emergent, but more than routine conditions. Finally, *minor emergency* center, summarizing acuity of presentation independent of the time factor involved in care.

Another point of distinction applies to operational practice as it relates to Centers for Medicare and Medicaid Services (CMS) billing guidelines.[3] The condition precedent is that at least one-third of visits are seen in this setting. The three stated criteria include patients seen: 1) on an urgent basis, 2) without an appointment and 3) for treating emergency medical conditions.

Therefore, the classification system dictates an *urgent care* center, usually free-standing, typically does not meet the third criteria, relaxing the EMTALA guidelines, but associated with decreased reimbursement as well.

The major distinction, however, is between the Type A facility—the typical 24/7 ED held out as an emergency center and utilizing emergency coding (99281–99285)—and the Type B facility—operating as an integral *fast track* center without the capability of caring for emergency cases associated with intermediate billing codes (G0380–0384). This compares to an integral *minor emergency* center that accepts all patients including those with lower acuity emergency conditions utilizing conventional emergency billing codes.

An average of 30%, with a range of 20–40% of patients, can be seen in the setting usually by a midlevel provider. Coincidentally, those patients with minor illnesses and accidents appreciate the attentive care that is provided by an enthusiastic midlevel practitioner. If nothing else, this physician extender, physician's assistant, or nurse practitioner can actually perform medical screening in some states that have by-law provisions to actually assist in redirecting inpatients to the proper care resource (Figure 27).

Figure 27. Triage Protocols

CATEGORIZATION OF PATIENTS

EMERGENT

LIFE THREATENING

This priority rating is utilized for patients presenting to the Emergency Department with conditions requiring immediate intervention to avoid loss of life or limb or to prevent permanent disability. ALL PATIENTS TRIAGED AS EMERGENT WILL BE TRIAGED IMMEDIATELY TO A BED IN THE EMERGENCY DEPARTMENT. This patient should never be left unattended. Reassessment is continuous.

EXAMPLES

Active Seizure
Airway obstruction
Alkaline/Acid exposure to eyes
Allergic reaction with respiratory compromise
Cardiopulmonary arrest
Chest pain with hemodynamic instability
Coma
Compound fracture (with compromised circulation)
Emergency Childbirth
Hyperpyrexia (>105.0 F)
Hypothermia (<95.0 F)
Life threatening arrhythmias
Major trauma (Level 1 Triage Protocol)
Major Burns
Massive / uncontrolled hemorrhage
Possible CVA (< 2 hrs. after onset of symptoms)
Severe respiratory distress (pulse ox < 90% with oxygen)
Severe head injury
Shock

This list is not all-inclusive and serves only as a guideline. Each patient's needs should be determined individually. The experienced triage nurse must combine advanced skills, knowledge, flexibility, and intuition to provide optimum triage.

Ivy K. O'Rourke, RN, BSN, CEN, MBA
Rads B. Vukmir, MD, JD, FCCP, FACEP

1

ECi

Emergency Consultants, Inc. ©2003

Emergency Consultants, Inc. is a corporation providing management and administrative support to limited liability partnership clients. It is not a direct provider of professional medical care services.

Reference 2

Figure 27. Triage Protocols (continued)

<u>URGENT</u>

SEVERE, BUT NOT IMMEDIATELY LIFE THREATENING

This priority rating is utilized for patients presenting to the Emergency Department requiring rapid but not immediate care. Patients categorized as urgent may be assessed at Triage. This patient will require therapeutic intervention within 5 - 60 minutes.

This patient should be seated in an area that will allow ongoing observation by the triage nurse. Comfort measures such as a pillow or stretcher should be provided as needed if possible. Vital signs should be reassessed as indicated by patient condition.

Examples

Abdominal / Flank pain (moderate to severe and/or abnormal vital signs)
Altered level of consciousness / Loss of consciousness
Asthma with respiratory distress (pulse ox <90 on room air)
Chest pain (hemodynamically stable)
Compound fracture (without circulatory compromise)
CVA / Stroke (> 3 hrs after onset of symptoms)
Dislocation (without circulatory compromise)
Drug ingestion (conscious, at low risk for sudden deterioration)
Eye injury (impaired visual acuity)
Gastro-intestinal bleeding (with stable vital signs)
Headache (severe pain, altered mental status, abnormal vital signs)
History of seizure
Lacerations with severe bleeding or neurovascular compromise
Lethargic child
Major epistaxis
Moderate burns
Patients with orthostatic vital signs
Respiratory distress (pulse ox < 90% on room air)
Severe pain
Vaginal bleeding (greater than normal menses, stable vital signs)

This list is not all-inclusive and serves only as a guideline. Each patient's needs should be individualized.

Ivy E. O'Rourke, RN, BSN, CEN, MBA
Pado B. Tukmir, MD, JD, FCCP, FACEP

2

ECi

Emergency Consultants, Inc. © 2004

Emergency Consultants, Inc. is a corporation providing management and administrative support to limited liability partnership clients. It is not a direct provider of professional medical care services.

Reference 2

Figure 27. Triage Protocols (continued)

<u>NON-EMERGENT</u>

STABLE

      This priority rating is utilized for patients presenting to the Emergency Department who are STABLE (not severe or life threatening). These patients require evaluation and treatment, but time is not a critical factor.

      Patients categorized as non-emergent are able to register themselves while waiting for care. They are taken to the treatment area by the next available nurse according to arrival time, unless their condition worsens. These patients should be reassessed at least every 2 hours.

EXAMPLES

Abscess (>2 cm. In diameter)
Ambulatory MVA
Asthma (no respiratory distress, pulse ox > 90% on room air)
Back pain (simple, moderate, <50 yrs. old, not involving fall from a height)
Cellulitis
Chronic Headaches
Croup (without stridor, retractions or respiratory distress)
Dislocation (finger or toe, no circulatory compromise)
Epistaxis (controlled)
Fever (exceeding Urgent Care criteria)
Laceration requiring sutures (not actively bleeding)
Mild abdominal pain with normal vital signs
Minor eye complaints
Nausea, vomiting, diarrhea (stable)
Penile lesions or discharge
Rash (without systemic symptoms)
Stabilized isolated extremity injury (without deformity)
Urinary tract infection symptoms
Urinary retention
Vaginal bleeding (less than or equal to normal menses)
Vaginal discharge (without fever or severe abdominal pain)
Vaginal spotting without pain

This list is not all-inclusive and serves only as a guideline. Each patient's needs should be determined individually.

Ivy K. O'Rourke, RN, BSN, CEN, MBA
Rade B. Vukmir, MD, JD, FCCP, FACEP

3

ECi

Emergency Consultants, Inc. ©2003

Emergency Consultants, Inc. is a corporation providing management and administrative support to limited liability partnership clients. It is not a direct provider of professional medical care services

Reference 2

Figure 27. Triage Protocols (continued)

FAST TRACK

NON-URGENT

This priority rating is utilized for patients presenting to the Emergency Department with conditions that are minor in severity. Extended waiting periods will not compromise patient outcome.

Patients categorized as non-urgent are able to register themselves while waiting for care. These patients will be taken to the treatment area when there is a room available. These patients should be reassessed at least every 4 hours.

EXAMPLES

Abrasions (resulting from minor injury)
Abscess (minor, < 2 cm. In diameter)
Back pain (chronic, simple)
Bites (not requiring sutures, debridement, extensive irrigation)
Blood alcohol requests
Cast checks (without circulatory compromise)
Catheter change
Cold symptoms (without respiratory distress)
Dressing change
Earache (without fever)
Fussy child
Ingrown toenail
Insect bites / stings (without systemic symptoms)
Lab requests
Minor laceration (not requiring sutures)
Medication request
Needlestick injury
Ring removal (without circulatory compromise)
Sore throat (without respiratory distress or drooling)
Splint check
Splinter removal
Subungual hematoma
Suture removal
Toothache

This list is not all-inclusive and serves only as a guideline. Each patient's needs should be determined individually.

Reference 2

Another approach is to supplement the midlevel practitioner with a primary care physician usually certified in family practice, medicine-pediatrics ideally or internal medicine in some cases, who can bridge the gap between urgent care and true emergencies. Their approach to family oriented care often works with the often complex multiple patient evaluation scenario. This leaves the ED physician more suitably matched to more acute critical illness patient encounters.

References

1. "Benchmarking in Emergency Services." *ACEP Management Course Manual* 1994: 7.

2. Emergency Consultants Inc.® Vukmir, R., O'Rourke, I. *QualChart Information Systems Patient Management Program.* Traverse City, MI. Revision 4.04; 2005–2006.

3. http://www.cms.hhs.gov/HospitalOutpatientPPS/downloads/OPPS_Q&A.pdf.

Chapter 13

The Admission Process

Current analysis of the admission process begins with historical patient processing experience. A 1978 study found that 91% of hospitals maintained an ED unit with a "voluntary" medical staff rotation in two-thirds of sites while 30% were a subcontracted call service.[1] This medical staff rotation was exhibited in smaller (<100 bed) hospitals (82%), while larger facilities (41%) used contracted physicians. Resident physicians were used in 30% of cases and 23% contracted staff physicians for coverage.

The proportion of overall admissions accounted for by the ED was 21–25% with a range of 16–30%. Interestingly, this was a difference based on the corporate ownership status of the facility. The not-for-profit (NFP) hospitals admitted 16–30% of patients through the ED on average, 45% in governmental hospitals, and the least 42% in investor-owned hospitals are admitted through the ED.

Now, the overall admission rate through the ED is 15% with a range of 8–30% based on age and acuity. The proportion of all hospital admissions that is processed through the ED is now 50–75% of the total. A trend toward direct primary and specialty care evaluation of insured patients in the ED, leaving undefined payor classes to receive conventional ED evaluation pathways, can occur in some cases.

The patient admission process has certainly become the paramount issue facing most ED care providers. The primary problem is one of financing of both the inpatient and outpatient encounter. The ever-burgeoning proportion of unfunded care causes progressive deterioration of the payor mix. In some office-based practices, existing patients often report that they are urged to go to the ED if outstanding, unpaid medical balances are present; the same thing sometimes also happens in the cases of new patients if an evaluation fee is lacking for some specialists.

A perhaps too-common scenario becomes the inability of the referral physician to assume responsibility for patient care as workloads become overwhelming.

The solution requires active participation of the administration through a facilitated operational and financial approach to encourage the physicians' obligation to provide follow-up, on-call care to ED patients encountered—in addition to the EMTALA-mandated requirements.

The reasons offered by some on-call physicians for their request for non-involvement center around the premise that the patient could be discharged from the ED. Their rationale is varied and often includes seemingly well-intended reasons for this decision (Figure 28).

First, they might suggest, for instance, that the ED physician is perhaps inexperienced, not knowledgeable enough, or too risk-avoidant to discharge the patient. Certainly, it is counterproductive to trade credentials, but EM is one of the more competitive residencies and its practitioners are usually well-qualified in evidenced-based medicine practice. Unfortunately, when performing their job capably, EM physicians can sometimes increase another practitioner's workload.

Next, there can be transference to the patient. The referral physician suggests that the patient may be unreliable—they don't follow up, or they are noncompliant with medications or other recommendations, and they have therefore been "fired" from the practice. Examination of state medical society guidelines finds that this rationale is not endorsed for discharging patients from one's practice.

Often times a well-intended approach can go awry, such as suggesting that a patient be discharged from the ED so that he can be seen in the office. This approach can be an EMTALA violation if the patient turns out to be "unstable." Obviously, this condition is usually diagnosed retrospectively, only after an untoward outcome has occurred in a patient who is discharged to "someone's office" for subsequent care, for which they may not be compliant.

A comprehensive approach is required to handle this multifaceted problem. First, it is necessary to ensure that the same standards exist for credentialing. Generally speaking, all physicians on staff who work in both inpatient and outpatient settings should have the same performance requirements expected and applied. Second, a protocolized and stan-

Figure 28. Rationale to Refer to Another Practice

Top reasons for a primary care or consultant physician to refer or transfer a patient—either on call for unassigned, or for pre-established relationship when not on call.

1. "The patient has an outstanding unpaid balance"
    - Lack of payment is not acceptable to transfer, must offer reasonable payment plan

2. "The patient is discharged from my practice"
    - Require 30 days written notice, usually by certified delivery method

3. "Although I practice as an orthopedist I have not done a hand fellowship"
    - Burden transfer to consultant to evaluate prior to transfer or arrange follow-up

4. "They did not make an office appointment after their last admission"
    - Office follow-up is not required for duty to treat relationship to stay intact

5. "They missed 2 office appointments"
    - Not valid discharge from practice criteria
    - Inquire about transportation, childcare needs
    - Involve social services to assist

6. "They haven't seen me in one year"
    - If upheld at all, requires 2- to 3-year hiatus according to medicaid in most states

7. "They have sued me in the past"
    - Filing court claim does not relieve care responsibilities

8. "They are non-compliant with my plan and recommendations"
    - Medical compliance is notoriously poor in some circumstances
    - Does not meet discharge unless longstanding practice of care refusal

9. "They belong to my partner"
    - Call coverage extends throughout medical group

(continued)

Figure 28. Rationale to Refer to Another Practice (continued)

10. "Yes, I am covering for physician X, but I don't have hospital privileges"
    - Requires notification of medical staff office for evaluation

11. "We don't see _____ disease patients"
    - Could result in discrimination claim as well

12. High acuity or chronic conditions such as dialysis
    - Require physician-to-physician transfer of care

13. Transfer of care provisions in certain lower acuity condition, such as pregnancy
    - Cannot transfer 3rd trimester patients presenting in labor

14. "Our office is not equipped for wheelchair-bound patients"
    - Potential Americans with Disability Act (ADA) discriminatory action

15. "They need a specialty doctor (GI, ID, Cardiology) for the problem"
    - EMTALA empowers ED provider to make appropriate referral

16. "They don't need to be admitted, send them home"
    - EMTALA empowers ED physician to make admission decision

17. "Her OB doctor is at a different hospital"
    - "Contractions are only 8 minutes apart"
    - EMTALA mandates no transfer case

18. "What kind of insurance do they have?"
    - Prohibited question

19. "I don't take X insurance"
    - Provide care, then post-care consideration

20. Refer to teaching service
    - Need valid non-financial reason as well as educational merit

dardized patient care guideline system helps to minimize these individual care discrepancies amongst practitioners.

These care events should be made externally reviewable using well-established patient care guidelines. Remember, internal peer review can sometimes be flawed due to various subjective issues or bias, and external explicit peer review is often crucial to deciding the proper course for the patient (Figure 29).

Remember, there can be a significant dichotomy in the "continuum" of patient care. The ED physician often strives for maximal sensitivity, attempting to eliminate significant errors of omission. On the contrary, the admitting physician is compelled to stress maximum specificity, attempting to minimize errors of commission. Therefore, the ED physician is compelled to not miss anything, while the admitting physician is forced to not admit any patient unnecessarily—a constant struggle.

Obviously, in the search for the proper balance between sensitivity and specificity or accuracy, the composite endpoint is most desirable. However, erring on the side of caution and admitting more patients than necessary is desirable on an individual basis from the perspective of the social good. However, on a macroeconomic basis, the medical system is potentially at a breakpoint in some areas and the additional cost of inappropriate admissions is difficult to tolerate.

Another slowdown to the admission process is the "One More Test" approach. Here, a perhaps "too complete" workup is suggested by one practitioner to help to refine the diagnosis or to solicit another physician or service to admit the patient instead. Here, an effective approach is to the make the admissions assignment to a primary service, while additional testing can be done during the admission to refine the diagnostic and treatment plan. It usually does not change the admission physician; and it usually does not change the patient's course in the subsequent care of the admission physician.

Occasionally, this scenario ends with a disagreement where the PCP wants the patient to be discharged from the ED without performing a medical evaluation. This forces the ED physician to take the majority, if not all, of the medicolegal responsibility for the patient discharge.

The EMTALA statute is definitive on this point, stating that the ED physician has the final word on the admission decision. However, if it is invoked too often, even in the patient's best interest, the ED physician can be suggested to be non-collegial.

Figure 29. ACS-Admission Guidlelines Telemetry Care

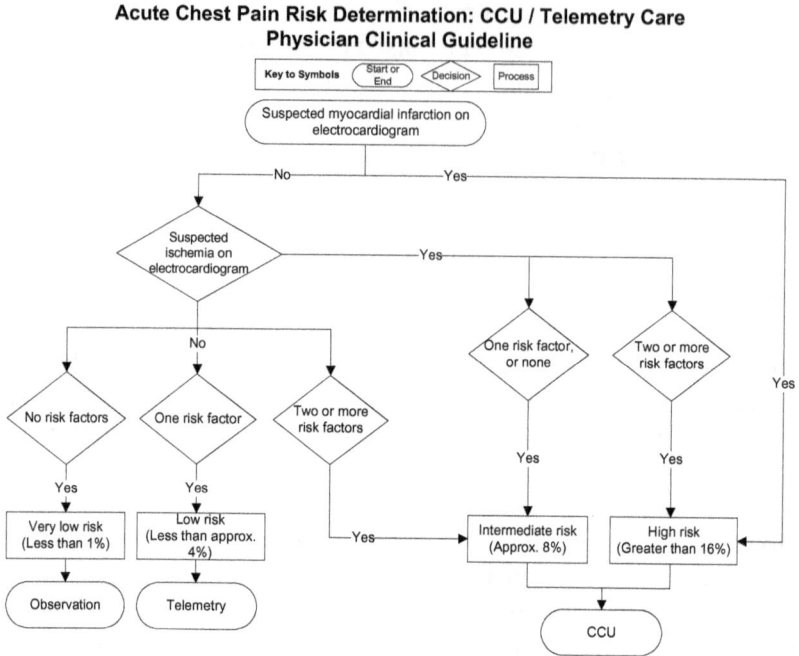

Acute Chest Pain Risk Determination: CCU / Telemetry Care Physician Clinical Guideline

DETERMINATION OF SHORT-TERM RISK OF FATAL OR NONFATAL MYOCARDIAL I INFARCTION:

LOW RISK *
Increased frequency, severity or duration of angina.

Angina provoked at a lower threshold.

New-onset angina with onset 2 wk to 2 mo before presentation.

Normal or unchanged electrocardiogram.

INTERMEDIATE RISK **
Prolonged (greater than 20 min) angina at rest, now resolved, with moderate or high likeli- hood of coronary artery disease.

Angina at rest (greater than 20 min or relieved with rest or sublingual nitroglycerin).

Nocturnal angina.

Angina with dynamic T-wave changes.

New onset Canadian Cardiovascular Class III or IV angina in the previous 2 wk with a moderate or high likelihood of coronary artery disease.

Pathologic Q waves or ST segment depression of < 1 mm in multiple lead groups (anterior, inferior, lateral) at rest.

Age greater than 65 yrs.

HIGH RISK ***
Prolonged (greater than 20 min) ongoing pain at rest.

Pulmonary edema, most likely related to ischemia.

Angina at rest with dynamic ST segment changes of greater than 1 mm.

Angina with new or worsening mitral regurgitation murmur.

Angina with symptoms or new or worsening rales.

Angina with hypotension.

Data are from the AHCPR guidelines for unstable angina in Braunwald et. al.
* To be considered at low risk a patient must have no features of the high-risk or intermediate risk patient and have at least one of the features described.
** To be considered intermediate risk, a patient must have no high-risk features and at least one of the features described.
*** To be considered at high risk a patient must have at least one of the features described.

Rade B. Vukmir, M.D., JD, FCCP, FACEP

Reference 2, 3

To avoid conflict, the ED physician should first reevaluate their own position to ensure its correctness (Figure 30). Then, it is proper to ask the PCP to evaluate the patient in person, since they often have more longitudinal knowledge of the patient history and condition. In the most extreme cases, there is a medicolegal requirement that the physician activate the administrative chain of command involving the department chair, as well as the administrator on duty or nursing supervisor who can also be helpful. The utmost care is required to not expose the patient or family to the difference in care plans between health care professionals. When in doubt, approach another service or facility to admit a patient or utilize a prolonged ED observation course if no other options are available to the physician.

Figure 30. Steps in Conflict Avoidance

Try these approaches when care discrepancies exist:

1. Try to recontact the physician a second or third time.
2. If necessary, ask them to present to evaluate the patient.
3. Contact an alternative specialty physician—cardiology for chest pain as an example.
4. Contact an alternative provider of the same specialty.
5. Contact the department chair person for assistance. Failure to do so results in additional legal liability for the ED physician, as the "chain of command" was not activated.
6. Enlist the assistance of nursing supervisor or administrator on duty to ensure patient care.
7. If all else fails, keep the patient in the ED for observation.
8. Only transfer to a higher level of care. Even a lateral transfer for financial reasons may incur an EMTALA claim.
9. If forced to transfer a patient, contact both the receiving admitting physician *and ED physician* prior to transfer.

References

1. Kessler, M.S., Wilson, K.C. "Emergency department key factor in hospital admissions." *Journal of the American Hospital Association* 1978; 52(24): 87, 90, 92 passim.

2. Emergency Consultants Inc.© Vukmir, R., O'Rourke, I. *QualChart Information Systems Patient Management Program.* Traverse City, MI. Revision 4.04; 2005–2006.

3. Braunwald, E., Mark, D.B., Jones, R.H., et al. "Unstable Angina: Diagnosis and Management." *Clinical Practice Guideline No. 10. AHCPR Publication No. 94-0602*; May 1994.

Chapter 14

The Consultation Process

Another potential pinch-point in the admission process is the referral of the patient from primary care to the specialist—or from the specialist to the sub-specialist—for further evaluation. Here, primary care may refer to cardiology for chest pain, to neurology for a transient isthemic attack (TIA), or an orthopedist might refer a hand injury to a hand specialist. This is often associated with further delay in patient processing as additional testing is often requested at this point as well by the specialist physician. Often it seems the testing is directed to refine the diagnosis and that would preclude admission to that service or compel admission to another service.

A potential remedy to this difficulty is built around a "One-Call Admission System" process. First, the primary care physician is contacted for evaluation and may then required to notify the consultant himself rather than to enlist the ED staff to perform this task (Figure 31). Secondly, the availability of advanced testing in the ED often encourages over-utilization in this setting to arrive at the proper diagnosis. Here, it is important to recognize the proper disposition–diagnosis dichotomy, with the ED physician most responsible for the former contribution, and the admitting physician the latter. It is clearly desirable that the patients are transferred to the floor to avoid further diagnostic testing. Then only significant positive testing results need to be referred to the ED physician for intervention after the patient is admitted.

The lack of specialty or sub-specialty availability has become an enormous conundrum in the world of emergency medicine. There are specific "Pay for Call" programs that have become firmly established in specific geographic regions and healthcare markets. Clearly, there is a

Figure 31. "One-Call Admission" Process

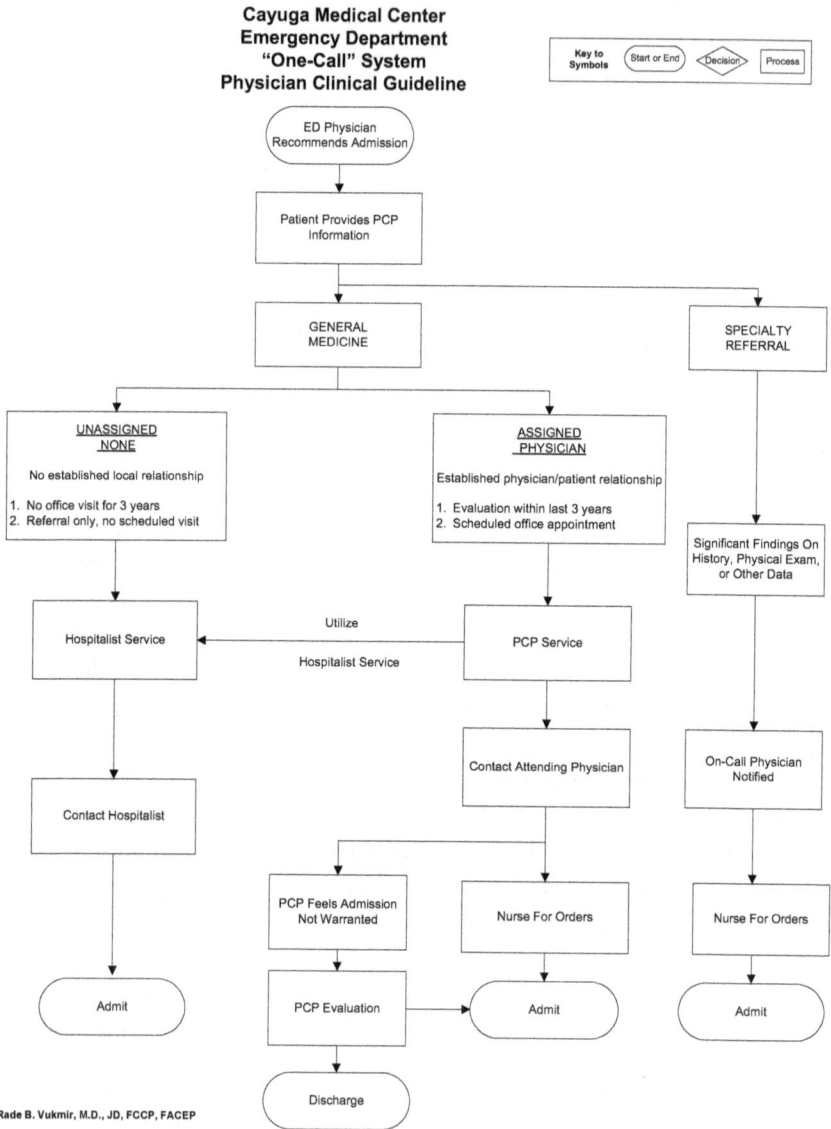

Cayuga Medical Center
Emergency Department
"One-Call" System
Physician Clinical Guideline

Key to Symbols: Start or End | Decision | Process

ED Physician Recommends Admission

Patient Provides PCP Information

GENERAL MEDICINE

SPECIALTY REFERRAL

UNASSIGNED NONE

No established local relationship

1. No office visit for 3 years
2. Referral only, no scheduled visit

ASSIGNED PHYSICIAN

Established physician/patient relationship

1. Evaluation within last 3 years
2. Scheduled office appointment

Significant Findings On History, Physical Exam, or Other Data

Hospitalist Service

Utilize
Hospitalist Service

PCP Service

Contact Hospitalist

Contact Attending Physician

On-Call Physician Notified

PCP Feels Admission Not Warranted

Nurse For Orders

Nurse For Orders

Admit

PCP Evaluation → Admit

Admit

Discharge

Rade B. Vukmir, M.D., JD, FCCP, FACEP

This clinical guideline is part of our education, quality management, and risk management program, and has been prepared by ECI for its partners and affiliates. Information contained herein addresses emergency medical practice in general. It is not a substitute for the hospital's policies and procedures nor the practitioner's knowledge and skill in the care and treatment of any individual patient. This information may be utilized as a guide to assist in a wide variety of circumstances and is not intended to establish a standard of care.

Emergency Consultants, Inc. © 2007

March 2007

Reference 1

desire to link risk and rewards of medical practice. This approach stresses the financial rewards over the intangible benefits of medical practice and in some regions appears to involve more specialty than primary care. Call systems where physicians are compensated for onsite evaluation and not the time period of coverage, and clinical protocols such as that for chest pain or other medical conditions may help as well (Figure 32).

Foremost, there is a moral obligation to provide call by the physician who derives a benefit from their hospital association. Simply put, if the hospital offers a service line, it must provide a reasonable call system and if the physician has hospital staff privileges, then they are somewhat obliged to provide on-call coverage. If there is no other recourse than to pay physicians to take call then the "employee model" is a desirable alternative. Here, the economic benefits of the employed physician far outnumber those associated with the "Pay for Call" approach. The employed physician is compelled to evaluate all patients referred without being selective. Unfortunately, in some "Pay for Call" programs, there is an opportunity to achieve the benefits of getting call pay, but not actually having to evaluate any patients during the call period. These programs perform better on a per capita basis where compensation is paid per onsite evaluation or admission rather than for phone consults alone.

There is another novel approach where the specialist now refers to the super-specialist. The most commonly encountered scenario would likely be an orthopedic or plastic surgery specialist who previously would have taken a hand injury, but now passes on a complicated hand injury, mainly because they did not complete a hand fellowship.

The question is a simplistic one—Is that patient better off in the hands of a specialist or the ED generalist for a complicated injury? Obviously, it is the former; even though the specific fellowship training was not done, they are still a specialist compelled by their own specialty board to handle that sort of problem, at least in general terms. The optimum approach for the patient is for the specialist to present and evaluate the case for potential referral to the sub-specialist physician. They then can assign and make transfer arrangements if warranted if there is any uncertainty on the ED physician's part concerning the care offered.

Often the consultant will ask that a complicated patient be admitted to the primary care physician, even with a specialty problem. The most common scenario is admitting a patient with a surgical or orthopedic problem who may not require imminent surgery due to a multiplicity of medical problems.

Figure 32. Chest Pain Admission Protocol

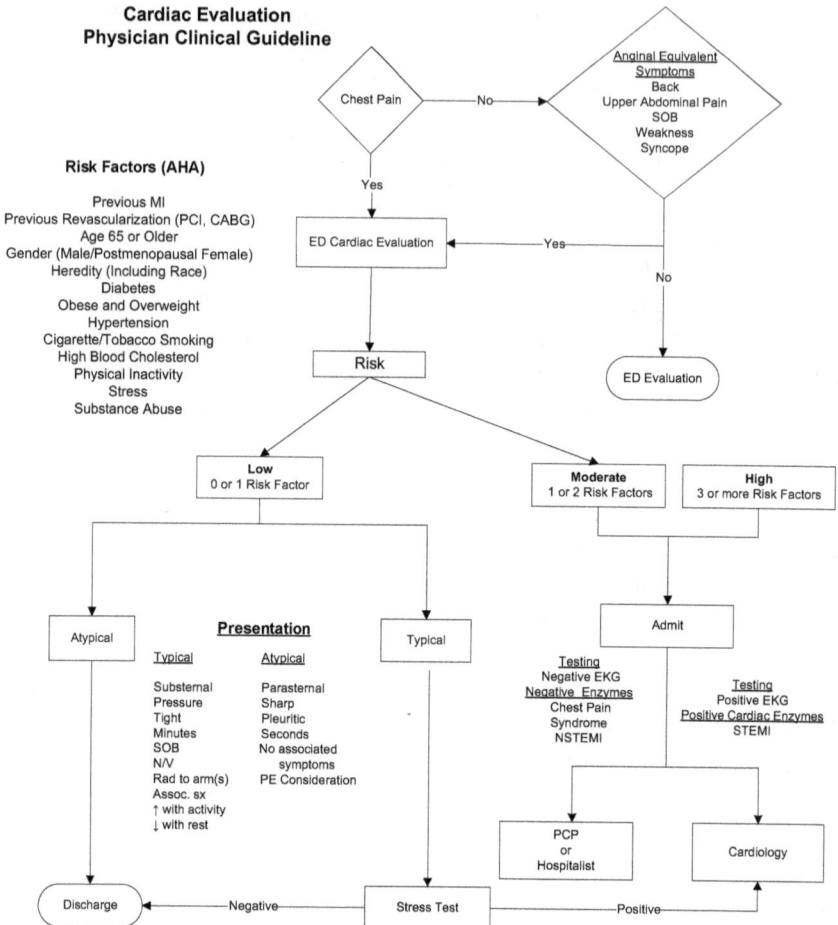

**Cardiac Evaluation
Physician Clinical Guideline**

Chest Pain — No — Anginal Equivalent Symptoms / Back / Upper Abdominal Pain / SOB / Weakness / Syncope

Risk Factors (AHA)

Previous MI
Previous Revascularization (PCI, CABG)
Age 65 or Older
Gender (Male/Postmenopausal Female)
Heredity (Including Race)
Diabetes
Obese and Overweight
Hypertension
Cigarette/Tobacco Smoking
High Blood Cholesterol
Physical Inactivity
Stress
Substance Abuse

Yes → ED Cardiac Evaluation ← Yes

No → ED Evaluation

Risk

Low 0 or 1 Risk Factor

Moderate 1 or 2 Risk Factors

High 3 or more Risk Factors

Atypical

Presentation

Typical	Atypical
Substernal	Parasternal
Pressure	Sharp
Tight	Pleuritic
Minutes	Seconds
SOB	No associated
N/V	symptoms
Rad to arm(s)	PE Consideration
Assoc. sx	
↑ with activity	
↓ with rest	

Typical

Admit

Testing
Negative EKG
Negative Enzymes
Chest Pain
Syndrome
NSTEMI

Testing
Positive EKG
Positive Cardiac Enzymes
STEMI

PCP or Hospitalist

Cardiology

Discharge ← Negative — Stress Test — Positive →

Sources:
AHA Scientific Statement. *Circulation* 2005; 111:2699-2710.
Stabilization of the patient with acute coronary syndromes. *Circulation* 2005; 112:89-110.

Rade B. Vukmir, M.D., JD, FCCP, FACEP

This clinical guideline is part of our education, quality management, and risk management program, and has been prepared by ECI for its partners and affiliates. Information contained herein addresses emergency medical practice in general. It is not a substitute for the hospital's policies and procedures nor the practitioner's knowledge and skill in the care and treatment of any individual patient. This information may be utilized as a guide to assist in a wide variety of circumstances and is not intended to establish a standard of care.

Emergency Consultants, Inc. © 2007

March 2007

Reference 1

This process can be avoided with clear admission guidelines for specialty disease entities, such as hip fractures (Figure 33). If the admission to primary care is desired, the specialist should make contact for this consultation as well.

Figure 33. Hip Fracture Protocol

	HIP FRACTURE TRANSITION ORDERS

ADMIT TO: DR. _____ Service: _____ ☑ Old charts to floor

DIAGNOSIS:
ADMIT STATUS: ☐ OBS (less than 24 hrs) ☐ Inpatient **BED TYPE:** ☐ General ☐ Monitored ☐ ICU ☐ Other _____
CODE STATUS: ☐ Full ☐ No intubation ☐ No CPR ☐ Chemical only ☐ Care and comfort only
VITALS: ☐ q 2 hr and prn ☐ q 4 hr and prn ☐ q shift and prn ☐ Other _____
ALLERGIES: ☐ NKDA _____
ACTIVITY: ☐ Ad lib ☐ BRP ☐ BRP with assist ☐ Restrictions: _____
DIET: ☐ NPO ☐ Clear Liquids ☐ Regular ☐ ADA_____ cal ☐ Other _____

NURSING:
☐ Intake and output q shift   ☐ _____
☐ Foley catheter or straight cath PRN if unable to void   ☐ _____
☐ Assess pain using numeric pain rating scale (0-10) q_____ hrs and PRN

IV FLUIDS:
☐ PRN adapter, flush per protocol   ☐ IV fluid @ _____ml/hr.   ☐ 0.9% NS ☐ D5 0.45% NS ☐ _____
☐ with _____ mEq KCl per 1000 ml. Not to infuse at rate greater than 10 mEq/hr

RESPIRATORY:
☐ O_2 by nasal cannula at 2-4 L/min (maintain pulse ox greater than 90%)   Notify physician if pulse ox less than 90% on O_2 4L/min
☐ Pulse oximetry ☐ Continuous   ☐ Every shift and PRN for shortness of breath
☐ May discontinue O_2 and O_2 sat if SaO_2 greater than or equal to 92% on room air
☐ Incentive spirometry: provide incentive spirometer with instructions for use - encourage to use 10 times per hour

MEDICATIONS: Weight _____ ☐ lb ☐ kg Height _____ in. ☐ See medication reconciliation form for home meds to be continued
☐ Promethazine ☐ 12.5mg ☐ 25 mg ☐ IV ☐ IM every 4 hours PRN for nausea *(If IV, dilute per facility policy prior to administration)*
☐ Morphine Sulfate ☐ 1 - 2 mg IV PRN q hour for pain greater than or equal to _____ / 10.
                    ☐ 3 - 4 mg IV PRN q hour for pain greater than or equal to _____ / 10.
   ☐ Hold if SBP less than 90 mm Hg , RR less than 10 per min. Notify physician if patient continues to rate pain greater than 3/10.
☐ Fentanyl (Sublimaze®) 50 - 100 mcg IV every 4 hours as needed for moderate to severe pain
☐ Hydromorphone (Dilaudid®)0.5 mg - 2 mg slow IV every 4 - 6 hours as needed for moderate to severe pain
☐ Ketorolac (Toradol®) ☐ 10 mg po ☐ 15 mg ☐ 30 mg ☐ IV ☐ IM every 6 hours as needed for pain
☐ _____   ☐ _____
☐ _____   ☐ _____
☐ _____   ☐ _____
☐ _____   ☐ _____
☐ _____   ☐ _____
☐ _____   ☐ _____
☐ _____   ☐ _____
☐ Smoking Cessation Counseling ☐ Offer nicotine transdermal patch topically every 24 hrs ☐ 7 mg ☐ 14 mg ☐ 21 mg
☐ Pneumococcal/Influenza Vaccine - screen and administer per protocol if appropriate
(No aspirin, NSAIDs, or Coumadin® unless specifically ordered by physician preop)

See page 2 for additional orders

These orders have been developed to improve legibility/efficiency and are not intended to establish a standard of care, clinical guideline, or protocol. They are being written at the request of the attending physician, who has assumed the care and treatment of this patient. All sections are optional and at the discretion of the attending physician.
These orders are void after 24 hours.

Date	Time	Physician Signature	Physician Name (print) or Lic #

Page 1 of 2 pages   Hip Fracture Transition Orders (Revised 03/2007)

Reference 1

Figure 33. Hip Fracture Protocol (continued)

	HIP FRACTURE TRANSITION ORDERS (pg 2)

LABS:
- ☐ CBC   ☐ with diff   ☐ with manual diff
- ☐ Metabolic Panel: ☐ Basic   ☐ Comprehensive
- ☐ Type and Screen
- ☐ PT   ☐ INR   ☐ PTT

- ☐ Urinalysis   ☐ w/ microscopic   ☐ w/o microscopic
- ☐ Culture if indicated
- ☐ _____
- ☐ _____

RADIOLOGY:
- ☐ CXR: ☐ Portable (AP)   ☐ PA & Lateral
- ☐ Hip   ☐ Right   ☐ Left
- ☐ Pelvis

- ☐ _____
- ☐ _____
- ☐ _____

EKG:
- ☐ EKG

- ☐ _____

DVT PROPHYLAXIS:
- ☐ TED hose   ☐ Pneumatic Compression Stockings
-    ☐ Both legs   ☐ Unaffected leg only
- ☐ Heparin 5,000 units sub Q ☐ q 8 hrs   ☐ q 12 hrs
- ☐ Enoxaparin 40 mg sub Q daily

ORTHOPEDIC:
- ☐ Bucks Traction _____ lbs to affected Leg

- ☐ _____

THERAPIES: Evaluate and treat:
- ☐ PT   ☐ OT   ☐ _____

- ☐ _____

CONSULT: _____
☐ Social Services/Case Management

NOTIFY DR. _____   ☑ on arrival to approve above orders   ☑ for further orders

☑ **CONTACT ADMITTING PHYSICIAN OR PCP UPON ADMISSION FOR ROUTINE MEDICATION ORDERS**

ADDITIONAL ORDERS:
- ☐ _____
- ☐ _____
- ☐ _____
- ☐ _____
- ☐ _____
- ☐ _____
- ☐ _____
- ☐ _____
- ☐ _____
- ☐ _____

These orders have been developed to improve legibility/efficiency and are not intended to establish a standard of care, clinical guideline, or protocol. They are being written at the request of the attending physician, who has assumed the care and treatment of this patient. All sections are optional and at the discretion of the attending physician.
These orders are void after 24 hours.

Date	Time	Physician Signature	Physician Name (print) or Lic #

In compliance with *42 CFR Section 456.60* *Certification/Recertification*, I certify that the level of care is based on medical necessity as documented within this medical record.	**Physician's Initials**	

Reference 1

Another dilemma is the potential for call transfer within the on-call group itself. This scenario manifests itself when a call physician is unable to assume care responsibility for a variety of reasons. These reasons include situations in which one partner might be on vacation, the group might be short-staffed, or the person on call has no privileges at that institution since they usually cover one another, or they are the only practitioner in the office.

An unofficial comment has existed to deal with this issue—the so-called "three specialist rule." Actually not endorsed by a statutory mandate, it has some grassroots support in the medical consultation community. This suggestion is that if there are three practicing physicians of a particular specialty, then a comprehensive 365/24/7 call system is feasible for the participants.

These recommendations take the variability out of the physician on-call system for the benefit of the patient and nursing staff.

Reference

1. Emergency Consultants Inc.© Vukmir, R., O'Rourke, I. *QualChart Information Systems Patient Management Program.* Traverse City, MI. Revision 4.04; 2005–2006.

Chapter 15

The Discharge Process

There is a supposition that emergency care is relatively expensive to provide, more so than other portions of the hospital care system. However, it is not uncommon for the primary care or urgent care clinic to refer patients from their door to the ER for care.

The lack of appropriate follow-up resources increases the ED return rate. It is critical to examine the rationale behind office or clinic to ED referrals—sometimes due to an outstanding bill, lack of follow-up after a previous referral, or a situation in which the patient didn't follow care recommendations. This issue has a significant adverse impact on efficiency overall. A cooperative approach ensuring physician-to-physician contact between clinics and ED can help to facilitate the referral.

The benchmark pharmacy TAT is 20 minutes for medication delivery, which can prolong the discharge process if routine medicines are prescribed unnecessarily.

It is crucial to recognize that EMTALA mandates specific follow-up procedures. If the hospital provides a clinical service line, then a reasonable call program is required. A good point at which to begin is an inquiry concerning a physician's request for notification when on call. Some physicians want to be called regarding all outpatient referrals, while others prefer to not be contacted unless the patient presents to the office.

Another patient-focused consideration is that some patients cannot afford transportation, medication, or childcare. It is incumbent upon us to assist patients in taking personal responsibility by facilitating public service involvement, therefore employing the ED case manager or social service personnel to help towards this endpoint.

The financial outlay incurred to employ a social-service-based ED case manager is repaid many times over in a large volume ED that evaluates over 50,000 patients annually, but also in a smaller department with especially complicated care of patients. Departments that "cross-cover" the ED with the general social service practitioner whose expertise lies with oncology or pediatrics sometimes have greater difficulty with the emergency department process. The presence of an ED case manager with a passion that is directed towards the underserved is invaluable to the operation.

It is suggested that up to one-third of the ED population may have a psychosocial underlay to their visit; these present most often in the overnight time period (12 midnight to 8:00 AM).[1] Such cases often involve psychiatric illness or drug abuse issues as well.[2] The capacity to arrange appropriate transportation, housing, or drug and alcohol rehabilitation resources can help the department's efficiency with the appropriate discharges, as well as managing the costs of the added social services deliveries.

Another area of concern is the epidemic of domestic violence, pediatric, or elder group abuse, since these patients often present to the ED as the last "safe haven" from harm. The ability to provide recognition, education, and intervention by a social service practitioner with expertise in this area can make a world of difference.

One of the greatest effects on ED efficiency is the discharge process itself. The discharge process is vastly remote from the ED—both in physical space, occurring in a distant hospital unit, as well as in time, often occurring days to weeks later. The key to this approach is a "Backwards Discharge Planning" process.

Here, new admissions can be accommodated in the hospital system with proper discharge planning. First, the process begins with a discharge concierge and waiting area where the physically able patients can be sent to a lounge with large screen TV, refreshments, and concierge services to manage medications, visiting nurses, home health, and oxygen therapy, while they wait. This eliminates the wait for the family from the ethereal "ride home" and frees the bedspace for the next patient. In lieu of this facility, the family is contacted the night before to ensure availability and avoid delay.

The housekeeping staff then goes into emergency mode to clean available beds for new occupants. This care should be specialized for rapid turnover and should obtain the same early departure when the job is complete to encourage maximal efficiency.

That day's discharge process should begin at the conclusion of the nursing report when the discharge plan is commenced or is communicated to the clinical administrator on duty (AOD). This plan is optimally communicated in a face-to-face meeting involving the hospital 'gatekeeper'—often an ICU-based physician, or the hospital major admitting primary care physician, or the anesthesiologist on call with firsthand knowledge of the day's operating room (OR) schedule. Here, appropriate planning can take place that will channel the admission and/or outflow to available beds, while still maintaining emergency beds for unpredictable emergency cases.

The presence of floor-based case managers can help to facilitate the discharge plan, balancing proper reimbursement strategies with the potential needs of the patient heading for home or other transitional care. With proper planning, the floor should always have available beds. Remember, the emergency department actually sees higher acuity patients; delaying admissions can result in catastrophic consequences with inadvertent delays—"due to another admission, the admission nurse is at lunch, or the bed is not clean." There is universal recognition that routine use of ED "hall beds" is not the definitive patient overflow management plan.

From the top down, the hospital personnel must recognize that keeping the ED open and available for the best care requires that other hospital components are maintained at maximal readiness. Hospitals would be well served to have more than one patient overflow unit, as well as processes in place to flex and adapt staffing patterns.

References

1. Larkin, G.L., Claassen, C.A., Pelletier, A.J., Camargo, C.A., Jr. "National study of ambulance transports to the United States emergency departments: Importance of mental health problems." *Prehospital and Disaster Medicine* 2006 Mar–Apr; 21(2 Suppl 2): 82–90.

2. El-Guebaly, N., Armstrong, S.J., Hodgins, D.C. "Substance abuse and the emergency room: programmatic implications." *Journal of Addictive Diseases* 1998; 17(2): 21–40.

Chapter 16

Academic/Teaching Institutions

The academic or teaching center offers special considerations and challenges regarding hospital and departmental efficiency. The combination of housestaff with medical students changes the efficiency dynamic immeasurably.

The large teaching institution may have 500–1000 inpatient beds with as many as 500–1000 staff physicians accompanied by 100–500 residents in training. This adds tremendous variability to the credentialing process, providing additional areas of uncertainty.

The residents themselves also have varying degrees of expertise and motivation. Remember, good training attracts the best quality housestaff, providing a more predictable work product. There is a commonly held belief that having housestaff provides greater efficiency. In fact, some staff physicians will not admit to a hospital without housestaff to write the orders and see the patient in the evening. This allows the attending physician to have a 9–5 workday practice within some limits if they wish.

Hospitals view them as a "bargain" as well. In 2008, the average salaries of the housestaff ($42,000) were one-half the cost of a midlevel practitioner ($72,000) and one-third that of an employed physician ($160,000). The housestaff have less rights than either other group in the workplace, and only recently has there been legislation to regulate housestaff work conditions.

In reality, the efficiency of these hospitals can be decreased with the additional layer of residents and in some cases fellow level decision-makers; they can facilitate the care process, but can often slow the patient care processing as well. This observation is often borne out in the prolonged ED average turnaround times [TAT] (2.5 versus 4.5 hours) or hospital length of stay (3.5 days versus 5.5 days).[1]

The Accreditation Counsel for Graduate Medical Education (ACGME) recommends a maximum faculty supervision rate of 4.5 residents per faculty member.[2] There is a medicolegal risk as well as if physicians-in-training are substituted for staff physicians. A large pediatric emergency department that increased attending physician coverage four-fold, from 7600 to 26,820 hours annually, was associated with a 42% decrease in malpractice cases.[1] They found an improvement in attending physician patient evaluation from 15 to 100% of cases. The total legal financial disbursements decreased from $807,500 (an average of $73,406 per closed claim) to $450,000 (an average $64,256 per closed claim) in 1987–90.

Obviously, the presence of full-time attending coverage in a pediatric ED appears to decrease the frequency of malpractice litigation, as well as the amount of claims disbursement.

Therefore, although there appears to be a cost savings, in fact additional supervisory staff can most often be employed to transfer the residents from a primary to the auxiliary care role.

The patient interface is an interesting one as well, spanning the spectrum of acceptance. A minority of patients and families are not accepting of the medical training system, "not wanting anyone to practice on them." Likewise, others are very happy to talk to residents and often enjoy the youthful enthusiasm of trainees and students and are proud of their "interesting case" status.

An interesting patient–physician interface was explored, examining senior ED resident preferences for their own personal healthcare. 75% of the residents stated that they were willing to be seen by unsupervised residents for minor illness or injury, 50% for moderate conditions, but only 20% for major conditions.[3] The willingness to be seen increased with a hypothetical 2-hour care delay, before an attending physician could be consulted.

Ironically, the residents who were willing to be seen by a midlevel provider was decreased at all levels of severity. This was modified in that 84% were willing to be seen by a non-physician if a subsequent physician exam would occur, but only 50% would allow care by a midlevel if there was no subsequent physician evaluation.

The dual standard issue raised is inherently obvious. Either way, it is helpful to understand the benefits and detriments of the addition of housestaff to the hospital care delivery system.

References

1. Press, S., Cantor, J., Russell, S., Jerez, E. "Full-time attending physician coverage in a pediatric emergency department: effect on risk management." *Archives of Pediatrics & Adolescent Medicine* 1994; 148(6): 578–81.

2. Accreditation Council for Graduate Medical Education (ACGME). *Emergency Medical Guidelines.* ACGME 2000–2007.

3. Larkin, G.L., Kantor, W., Zielinski, J.J. "Doing unto others? Emergency medicine residents' willingness to be treated by moonlighting residents and nonphysician clinicians in the emergency department." *Academic Emergency Medicine* 2001; 8(9): 886–92.

Chapter 17

Risk Management

The balance point of operations is the interplay between efficiency and the likelihood of error. It is inherently obvious that the faster the patients are evaluated, the more the accompanying risk of error may increase once a maximum efficiency point is reached. This dilemma is often the precise focus of this particular transition point.

There are clear correlates of physician supervision and nurse staffing on patient outcome. The likelihood of mortality is increased for weekend versus weekday admissions (OR= odds ratio 1.28).[1] This increase was noted in 25% of the 100 most commonly admitted high-risk candidates. In fact, not one potentially fatal condition was found more common during the weekday.

The trend was further analyzed by referencing both an increased incidence and mortality associated with Friday discharge for the hospital.[2] The preemptive weekend discharge approach found Friday the most common discharge day (20%) compared to Saturday (12%) or Sunday (8%). Also, there were 5.4% of patients readmitted with 1.7% mortality at 30 days in the Friday discharge cohort (Figure 34).

Therefore, we should be cognitive of a tendency towards perhaps premature weekend discharge, decreased physician weekend rounding, decreased nursing staffing, and decreased housestaff supervision required in the weekend time period.

The key to this process allows the ED to control its own destiny. They are best able to determine this ED saturation point and the need to assume some control of other hospital operations, usually through the nursing supervisor—such as admission transfers and personnel decisions.

Figure 34. Discharge by Day of the Week

Day of Week	Discharge Proportion (%)	Hazard Ratios Death or Readmission
Monday	15	< 1.0
Tuesday	15	< 1.0
Wednesday	15	< 1.0
Thursday	15	1.00 *
Friday	20	1.04 *
Saturday	12	< 1.0
Sunday	8	< 1.0

Reference 2

This manifests itself as shunting "ED evaluations"—presumably having made contact with their physicians—to be admitted directly to the hospital, bypassing the ED. Likewise, patients with pre-established physicians or clinic relationships can be referred to that resource (cognizant of EMTALA considerations) usually requiring a physician or midlevel extender evaluation.

This may well dictate the additional use of adjunct resources such as lab, x-ray, or surgical resources. This is especially problematic from a financial perspective; shunting patients away from the ED should be avoided at all costs since outpatient testing has a positive financial impact on the institution.

Perhaps, the most helpful operational approach is the "Take Out" approach, where the floor staff comes to retrieve their patients when especially busy. Again, it is the house supervisor that has the bird's eye view of all resources and often has the credibility to get the difficult mission accomplished. Of course, this resource cannot be invoked inappropriately by the ED staff because the adverse effect on floor efficiency can be devastating. This false alarm phenomenon will not help to solidify relationships between the emergency department and the hospital medical ward staff.

The threat of malpractice litigation is often the most influential factor on ED operations as a whole. The effects are more multifaceted than they appear.[3, 4] First, the primary care office is more prone to send problematic high-risk patients to the ED, which increases evaluation time and the complexity of the "average" ED patient.

Second, the triage nurse is often compelled to transfer a patient from the urgent care internally to the ED because it is "too complicated." Often times in reality it is not more complicated per se, but more likely it is just time-consuming, such as in the case of abdominal or pelvic pain or pediatric illness in the very young, especially the less than 1-year-old age group.

Thirdly, risk avoidance strategy transfers to the ED physician the responsibility for often instituting multiple layers of sequential testing often at the request of the PCP to arrive at the proper diagnosis. Often times this additional refinement can be ordered, but completed after admission, assuming the most complicated diagnosis for bed assignment. Further, refinement can result in the bed status being adjusted to lower or higher levels of care as warranted.

Often the suggestion is made to transfer the patient to a tertiary or quaternary hospital, typically to a higher level of care. It is imperative that to engage in the risk of the transfer, clear benefit to the patient be demonstrated. The active involvement of the admitting physician in the transfer is sometimes imperative.

In more complicated cases, this may mean presenting for evaluation and contacting the referral physician to make the transfer themselves if there are discrepant opinions about the care plan. This would be required only for the most unusual of cases however. Hopefully, the great majority of time there is unified patient decision-making regarding patient care by all members of the team.

Remember, the goal of the system is to provide safe and effective care for all patients by the entire continuum of care. Participants should be delivered care in an interrelated fashion throughout the care chain in ideal circumstances. The ED is often the entry point to the care chain, but not necessarily the defining moment.

It has been suggested that there is a minimal effect of the ED on the overall costs of the healthcare system. A study was done comparing these with high and low "fear" of medical malpractice and subsequent risk aversion in university and a community hospital setting.

Those ED physicians in the risk averse group were less likely to discharge low-risk patients (64 vs 81%, OR 0.34), more often admit to a monitored or ICU bed (51 vs 42%, OR 1.7), and utilize greater troponin testing (80 vs 74%, OR 1.9) or chest radiography performance (OR 2.0).[4]

Therefore, there can be an adverse impact on efficiency when the most risk averse ED physicians treat the highest risk by incidence emergency condition—chest pain.

References

1. Bell, C.M., Redelmeier, D.A. "Mortality Among Patients Admitted to Hospitals on Weekends as Compared with Weekdays." *New England Journal of Medicine* 2001; 345(9): 663–8.

2. Van Walraven, C., Bell, C.M. "Risk of death or readmission among people discharged from hospital on Fridays." *Canadian Medical Association Journal* 2002; 166(13): 1672–3.

3. Press, S., Cantor, J., Russell, S., Jerez, E. "Full-time attending physician coverage in a pediatric emergency department: effect on risk management." *Archives of Pediatrics & Adolescent Medicine* 1994; 148(6): 578–81.

4. Katz, D.A., Williams, G.C., Brown, R.L., Aufderheide, T.P., Bogner, M., Rahko, P.S., Selker, H.P. "Emergency physicians' fear of malpractice in evaluating patients with possible acute cardiac ischemia." *Annals of Emergency Medicine* 2005; 46(6): 534–5.

Chapter 18

Emergency Department Efficiency Analysis

The various components of the emergency department patient care processing protocols have been reviewed independently, but legitimate analysis requires synthesis and valid benchmarking to be meaningful.

An early analysis from 1987 found delay in those with "routine and relatively minor" problems. They found an average delay in seeing the physician at 40 minutes for those with minor problems, 30 minutes for urgent, 10–15 minutes for critical but hemodynamically stable patients and a negligible delay for those requiring resuscitation[1] (Figure 35). They attributed this delay to the availability of fixed resources such as ready beds, clerks, and nursing, but left no recommendations concerning physician behavior as an etiology of delay.

Figure 35. Time to Physician Evaluation Delay

Time to Physician (minutes)
40 minutes	Minor complaints
30 minutes	Urgent
10-15 minutes	Critical and stable hemodynamics
0 minutes	Resuscitation

Reference 1

They also analyzed process variables such as those found with lab and x-ray. The treatment times were 30–40 minutes with no tests ordered, 45 minutes with urinalysis, 65 minutes with x-ray, and 126 minutes if blood testing was warranted (Figure 36).

Figure 36. Historical Processing Delay Associated with Testing

Testing Delay (minutes)

30-40 minutes	No testing
45 minutes	Urinalysis
65 minutes	X-ray
126 minutes	Blood testing

Reference 1

Efficiency suggestions to improve patient flow would be: First, improvement of laboratory turnaround time (TAT); Second, limitation of nonessential blood work on minor patients; Third, walk-in crisis for those with minor problems; and fourth, expansion of staffing during peak hours (Figure 37).

Figure 37. Steps to Maximize Efficiency

1. Improvement of laboratory turnaround time (TAT).
2. Limitation of nonessential blood work or x-ray testing on minor patients.
3. Walk-in clinics for those with minor problems.
4. Expansion of staffing during peak hours.

Reference 1

The next step would be to define benchmark data in a site-specific way to define an interventional plan. Another benchmark trial during the same time period found registration time shortest (17 minutes), in small community hospitals and longest (47 minutes) in a large urban ED sites.[2] The average time from registration to admission was 3 hours, usually due to lack of available beds.

Specific focus on radiology finds that an x-ray was performed on 40–50% of patients with an average time of 44 minutes from request to receipt of results. Factors associated with radiology turnaround time (TAT) include hospital size, time of day, proximity of radiology department, and technician availability (Figure 38).

Figure 38. Effects on Radiology Turnaround Time

1. Hospital size
2. Time of day
3. Proximity of radiology department
4. Technician availability

Reference 2

There were two interesting findings. First, interestingly, the delay from ED x-ray was longer on the day shift due to a conflict with regularly scheduled outpatient radiology procedures. Second, there were disproportionately smaller numbers of x-ray filming units allocated to the ED even though the department was responsible for one third of all procedures.

The average TAT for laboratory tests was 55 minutes performed in 30% of ED patients. The most efficient operation received a matching of resources and patient volume. They experienced 40% of daily ED visits on the day shift and 45% during the evening and 15% at night with peak volume at noon and 6:00 pm (Figure 39).

Figure 39. Proportion of patients related to the time of presentation

Shift	Patients Presenting (%)	Peak
Day	40	12 noon
Evening	45	6 PM
Night	15	—

Reference 2

The process of obtaining the benchmark radiology and laboratory times is crucial to effective ED operation.

An outdated, academic model was a particularly unique analysis of rate-limiting factors. A specific pediatric facility was evaluated during peak visit times (3–10 pm) when only 35% of patients were seen within

30 minutes of arrival and 155 minutes spent in the ED overall.[3] The mean timeframe from registration to room was 26 minutes, followed by an average 18-minute wait for the physician and an overall time from registration to physician contact of 49 minutes.

The wait for exam room placement was attributed first to lack of nurse availability, followed by scarcity of bedspace. The wait after room placement was then contingent upon physician availability, followed by quantity of clinical activity in the system (Figure 40).

Figure 40. Reasons for Patient Delay

Registration to Bedspace
1. Nurse Availability
2. Room Availability

Bed Placement to Physician Evaluation
1. Physician Availability
2. Facility clinical activity (busy factor)

Reference 3

An attempt at benchmarking should focus on the target activity or duration of physician interaction; the average overall physician service time per patient was 24.2 minutes (95% CI 23.1–25.3)—essentially equivalent to ACEP's 22 minutes per patient recommendation.[4]

There was wide variability based on patient acuity, with 9.8 minutes for walk-in patients, 25.0 minutes for laceration repair, 31.9 minutes for critical care, and 55.6 minutes for those patients maintained in observation status.

There was great diversity in the number of physician–parent interactions as well. The number of discrete physician bedside encounters was 1.1 visits for laceration repair, 1.3 for walk-in patients, 2.2 for non-selected "average" patients, 2.6 for critical care, and 6.3 for ED observation patients (Figure 41). Overall, the ED observation patient is the most time-consuming of all.

This study raises the valid issue of case mix when planning departmental needs and workforce assignment. There is additional benchmark efficiency regarding customer service, related to the "average" number of patient encounters expected per patient.

Figure 41. Discrete Physician Bedside Encounters by Visit Type

Visit Type	Visits
Laceration Repair	1.1
Walk-In	1.3
Average (unselected)	2.2
Critical Care	2.6
ED Observation	6.3

Reference 4

The expected benchmark therefore is 2 encounters per patient visit, including the initial evaluation and the discharge encounter. Additional patient interaction is always desirable, but may be limited by patient acuity and physician availability. The last issue notes the exponential increase in patient encounters required in an observation setting. The patient care and financial benefits need to be balanced by the additional resources needed.

Prior to instituting any work efficiency departmental plan, a revision of ED benchmarks is imperative. A benchmark TAT is 2.25 hours average, 1.0 hours for fast track, and 3.25 hours for admission patients.[5]

Another model reported similar findings, with an average TAT of 140 minutes, with 180 minutes for emergent, 150 minutes for urgent, and 60 minutes for non-urgent cases (Figure 42).

Figure 42. Turnaround Time (TAT) Benchmarking

TYPE	TIME
Emergency Consultants, Inc.©	
Average	2.25 hours
Fast Track	1.0 hours
Admission	3.15 hours
ACEP (American College of Emergency Physicians) Management Course	
Average	140 minutes
Emergent	180 minutes
Urgent	150 minutes
Non-urgent	60 minutes

Reference 6, 7

The next consideration is a time-certain analysis that specifies recommended milepost benchmarks on the ED journey. The range of recommendations can be grouped as time intervals or cumulative totals.

The interval milepost approach begins with the patient obtaining room access by 15 minutes and then 75 minutes from MD assessment to final disposition[6, 8] (Figure 43). Likewise, the cumulative timing approach ranges from door to intervention or treatment time of 49 minutes extending to 272 minutes from door to admission time.

Figure 43. ED Milepost Benchmarker

	BENCHMARK (minutes)	
Milepost	**Interval**	**Evaluations**
Room Access	15	—
Door to Physician	15	—
Door to Intervention/Treatment	—	49
MD Assessment to Disposition	—	75
Disposition to Discharge/Admission	—	86
Disposition to Discharge	15	—
Disposition to Admission	60	—
Arrival to Discharge	—	145
Arrival to Admission	—	272

Reference 6, 7

Lastly, the benchmark data should be compared at a specific institution often utilizing a time study. This allows individual nuances in healthcare delivery systems to be explored (Figure 44).

Various interventional models have been proposed to help to streamline the emergency department care process. A 15-step quality improvement intervention process was instituted, resulting in improved registration time, time to disposition, and time to discharge[9] (Figure 45).

However, performance was worsened in presenting patients to ED bedspace and subsequent hospital admission at times of peak census due to decreased staffing; this was indicated by a lack of ED bed availability in 30% and inpatient beds in 51% of cases.

It is important to note that these interventions were established over time in response to multiple efficiency studies. Also, improvement was not always noted and was not typically associated with "high census, low staffing" scenarios.

Figure 44. ED Time Study

Emergency Department Time Study
November 24, 1999

Time Lapses	Average (minutes)	Range (minutes)
Arrival to RN Assessment	7	0- 50
Arrival to MD Assessment	11	0 -57
Assessment to Labs Ordered	17	2-43
Assessment to Lab Results	41	19-60
Assessment to X-rays Ordered	17	2-67
Assessment to X-ray Results	62	2-120
Results to PCP Notified	26	2-75
PCP Notified to Orders	14	3-60
Orders to bed requested	28	1-120
Bed requested to Report	15	1-35
Report to Patient bed	26	4-75
Results to Patient to bed (no PCP info)	48	18-90
Results to Discharge	22	5-57

Average LOS—Treat and Discharge	1.8 hours
Average LOS—Admission	3.1 hours
Average time from orders to admit to bed	1.2 hours

Reference 10

Another model utilized a multi-disciplinary process improvement team focusing on registration, triage, staffing, radiology, laboratory testing, and bed availability (Figure 46).

The ED volume increased 17%, while the ED waiting room time then decreased from 31 to 4 minutes, a decrease of 83%.[11] The ED throughput intervals (triage to disposition time) decreased 27% for admissions and 31% for discharged patients, accompanied by a 92% reduction in patients who left without being seen, and improved patient satisfaction.

A critical review of this program finds an astonishing sevenfold improvement in waiting room time, thus raising questions about sustainability of improvement. It appears that they implemented a bedside registration standby, eliminating waiting room stays if bedspace was available—more of a "redesign" than improvement.

Figure 45. 15-Step Efficiency Plan

Time Interval	Baseline	Intervention
Improvement		
Presentation-Registration		
Completion	2.6 hours	2.3 hours
Medical Assessment		
Disposition Onset	2.3 hours	1.8 hours
Disposition Order		
Patient discharge	30 minutes	5 minutes
Worsening		
Registration Completion		
Treatment Area Entry	29 minutes	65 minutes
Disposition Order		
Hospital Admission	95 minutes	220 minutes

Reference 11

In conclusion, efficiency modification procedures require being cognizant of a number of limitations. First, properly define your objectives, know what you are analyzing. A sample ED efficiency redesign template has been included[11] (Figure 46). Second, standardize the objectives of measurement to improve the validity of both internal and external comparisons. Third, clarify the difference between redesigning a completely new process compared to improving upon an existing one. Fourth, one should memorialize steps and objectives achieved. Fifth, create a true multi-disciplinary team of people that do the work combined with those who affect the change.

Figure 46. ED Efficiency Redesign Template

1. Patient intake
2. Registration
3. Processing
    Lab
    X-ray
4. Staffing Model
    MD/Medical
    RN/Ancillary Staff
5. Data Processing
6. Physical Plant
7. Admission
8. Consultation
9. Discharge

Reference 11

Sixth, acknowledge individual contributions as well as group effort. Most importantly, make change permanent and revisit frequently to avoid aberrant regression of behavior.

References

1. Saunders, C.E. "Time study of patient movement through the emergency department: sources of delay in relation to patient acuity." *Annals of Emergency Medicine* 1987; 16(11): 1244–8.

2. Cue, F., Inglis, R. "Improving the operations of the emergency department." *Journal of the American Hospital Association* 1978; 52(13): 110–113, 119.

3. Liptak, G.S., Super, D.M., Baker, N., Roghmann, K.J. "An analysis of waiting times in a pediatric emergency department." *Clinical Pediatrics* 1985; 24(4): 202–9.

4. Graff, L.G., Wolf, S., Dinwoodie, R., Buono, D., Mucci, D. "Emergency physician workload: a time study." *Annals of Emergency Medicine* 1993; 22(7): 1156–63.

5. Emergency Consultants Inc.© "Group Utilization." *Vital Signs* 2006: B-4.

6. "Benchmarking in Emergency Services." *ACEP Management Course Manual* 1994: 7.

7. *Benchmark ED Staffing Ratios Based on Facility Size.* VHA Database, 2001.

8. Berger, R.G., Kichak, J.P. "Computerized physician order entry: helpful or harmful?" *Journal of the American Medical Informatics Association* 2004; 11(2): 100–103.

9. Kyriacou, D.N., Ricketts, V., Dyne, P.L., McCollough, M.D., Talan, D.A. "A 5-year time study analysis of emergency department patient care efficiency." *Annals of Emergency Medicine* 1999; 34(3): 326–35.

10. *Northwest Emergency Department Time Study*, November 24, 1999.

11. Spaite, D.W., Bartolomeaux, F., Guisto, J., Lindberg, E., Hull, B., Eyherablide, A., Lanyon, S., Cross, E.A., Valenzuela, T.D., Conroy, C. "Rapid process redesign in a university-based emergency department: decreasing waiting time intervals and improving patient satisfaction." *Annals of Emergency Medicine* 2002; 39(2): 168–77.

Chapter 19

Administration

Perhaps the most common miscategorization of the ED is as a "cost center." As discussed previously, the ED should more accurately be viewed as a "profit center" that is responsible for as many as 75% of hospital admissions. There is also a huge contribution to the charges rendered from the ED-based lab and x-ray work product.

A balance of these two views holds that the ED doesn't cost as much as you may think. Every dollar spent is an investment that spreads throughout the facility, paying dividends in other patient care arenas.

Another common myth is that the ED doesn't provide good customer service. On the contrary, a host of ED programs have touted customer service attributes for years. The nature of the ED population—with no prior physician relationship, uncertain medical conditions, and psychosocial stressors—often place the patient in a difficult situation. There is a corporate business adage that says that 2–3% of customers cannot be satisfied and the same ratio may exist in the emergency department. Actually, in emergency medicine it is much less with a 3–5 patient per 1000 complaint ratio as a reasonable estimate.[1]

In fact, they suggest that trying to achieve complete satisfaction in this group could even be detrimental to the staff morale overall. The remaining patients might be better served if the staff would devote their time and effort to them because there would be a greater chance of mutually positive patient interaction. There are a number of staff customer service programs available for this purpose.

This difficult ER "problem patient" strategy should undergo internal monitoring first since the ED staff can effectively self-police because they intimately understand the issues better than anyone. The synopsis of cases should be forwarded to the patient care committee for oversight and assistance with an objective improvement plan.

The cornerstone of the operation and the area often requiring the most administrative support is a properly functioning primary and specialty care call system. This program is essential to the optimum functioning of the department.

Remember, this is a hospital-wide issue rather than characterized as merely an ED issue. The ED is providing a service to the primary care and specialty community, providing a preliminary evaluation of patients presenting to the hospital for care. In some cases definitive care can be provided in the ED and in some cases it is a first step in the care continuum requiring admission and additional care. The patient care community serves the best interest of the patients, not the ED proper.

Reference

1.   Culhane, D.E., Harding, P.J. "Quality in customers: Great expectations." Presented to the American College of Emergency Physicians Management Academy, Practice Management Committee; 1994; Boston, Massachusetts.

Chapter 20

Conclusion

The maximally efficient and optimally effective ED can be better understood using a compartmentalized approach: First, by evaluating the patient intake registration and triage process. Second, by knowing that the patient is paramount both in demographics and processing. Third, the staff efficiency must include physicians and midlevel nurses, as well as the optimized use of auxiliary staff.

The logistic support offered by data processing in the physical plant itself is analyzed next. Perhaps the most work- and resource-intense areas are the admission, consultation, and discharge process. Lastly, teaching institutions require a separate and distinct analysis due to their uniqueness.

The significance of an efficiency program falls away if the medical oversight management strategies are not focused on the integrated patient care process[1] (Figure 47).

Figure 47. ED Efficiency Modification Program Limitations

1. Define your objectives.
2. Standardize your mileposts.
3. Clarify re-design vs. improvement.
4. Memorialize steps and objectives.
5. Utilize multidisciplinary groups.
6. Individual and group credit.
7. Make change permanent
8. Revisit process frequently.

Reference 3

Error analysis is facilitated by a structural analytic approach, evaluating information gathering, processing, confirmation, and communication[2] (Figure 48).

Figure 48. Factors Associated with Medical Misdiagnosis

Information Gathering	**Examples**
Faulty data Gathering	Insufficient history to make diagnosis
Failure to gather new data	New symptoms not factored into diagnosis
Clinical issues	Omitted physical exam areas
Information Processing	
Insufficient knowledge or skill	Test misinterpretation
Faulty information processing	Misattribute symptoms to another diagnosis
Confirmation	
Failure to verify diagnosis	Diagnosis not compared to test results
Failure oversight of care system	Failure of radiology call back system
Comparison	
Failure to communicate test results	Biopsy report lost
Lack of follow up	No referral resources available for ED referral

Adapted from Reference 1, 2

Lastly, the administrative support for all of these individual discrete units is the glue providing a cohesive united function to allow maximum efficiency of all centers of operation. A "Top Down" administrative approach ideologically and functionally is crucial to the success of the operation.

References

1. Landro, L. "Preventing the Tragedy of Misdiagnosis." *Wall Street Journal,* November 29, 2006.

2. Department of Veterans Medical Affairs Center. "Dropping the Ball: Diagnostic Errors." Northpoint, NY; State University of New York, Stonybrook 2006.

3. Spaite, D.W., Bartolomeaux, F., Guisto, J., Lindberg, E., Hull, B., Eyherablide, A., Lanyon, S., Cross, E.A., Valenzuela, T.D., Conroy, C. "Rapid process redesign in a university-based emergency department: decreasing waiting time intervals and improving patient satisfaction." *Annals of Emergency Medicine* 2002; 39(2): 168–77.

About the Author

Rade B. Vukmir, MD, JD is president of Critical Care Medicine Associates, a medical service and consulting enterprise founded in 1991. He is trained in emergency medicine and critical care medicine, and has a legal degree with a specialization in health law.

This company has been successful over the last eighteen years providing a wide variety of clinical medical activity, education, medicolegal services, and business consultation services.

Dr. Vukmir has authored over forty journal articles. Previous books published include *Care of the Critically Ill* (Parthenon Press) and *Airway Management in the Critically Ill* (Parthenon Press) in the medical genre.

Dr. Vukmir's third publication is a historical non-fiction novel entitled *The Mill* (University Press of America) This latter work addresses the changing business environment of an aging steel industry and its impact on the day-to-day lives of the inhabitants of its once thriving industrial town. *Lessons Learned: Successful Management in a Changing Marketplace* (University Press of America) attempts to unite a wide variety of work experience and business principals.

His most recent books, *The ER: A Year in the Life* (Hamilton Books) and *ER: One Good Thing a Day* (Rowman & Littlefield Publishing Group) attempt to relate to the reader both the joys and sadness encountered taking care of patients, families, and each other in the emergency department.

www.ingramcontent.com/pod-product-compliance
Lightning Source LLC
Chambersburg PA
CBHW031812190326
41518CB00006B/308